Media Literacy

An essential guide to the critical thinking skills for our complex digital world.

Nick Pernisco

Editor, www.UnderstandMedia.com

Los Angeles, CA / Seattle, WA / New York, NY

Contents

Preface

Different people define media literacy in many different ways. Academics sometimes like to say that media literacy is a framework for understanding the media's messages, biases, and effects. Media literacy educators sometimes define media literacy as the ability to access, analyze, evaluate, and create media in all its forms. Still others define media literacy as a simple awareness of the media we consume. They are all correct.

No matter how you define media literacy, or how much you understand about its origins or theories, media literacy is not difficult to learn. Not only can it be very simple to learn, it is a simple skill that can be improved upon over time, helping us become more media literate as time goes on.

While the ideas behind media literacy are taught in classrooms around the world, it is a basic concept and skill that is best used in the real world. The essential elements of critical thinking skills can be taught in a classroom, distilling lessons down to their most essential pieces, deconstructing a piece of media for in-depth study and reflection. However, it is the practice of these skills in real world situations, such as watching a 15-second advertisement on Hulu, which disappears before we have had an opportunity to think about what we just saw, is where the practice of media literacy truly shines.

Media literacy is a skill that should be learned by all people in a civil, democratic society. This was the impetus behind helping to design a media literacy course and teaching it for many years at Santa Monica College. I saw this as an important first step in bringing critical thinking skills about media to everyone in the world – a lofty goal, but quite possible, since media literacy is a continuum, not an on/off switch. This means that by planting the seed of the idea that media should be thought about critically, we can grow a tree of critical thinking over our lifetimes. This is true for anyone – ask someone to question their media choices and watch them rationalize their choice to themselves. The seed has been planted – they can decide to go down the media literacy rabbit hole, or ignore it and go back to living life as they had before.

This book has evolved over the years, edition by edition, adding and modifying material so that the concepts could reach as many people as possible. That is still the goal with the book, "Practical Media Literacy." And while this book has been reworked to be more of a text in an undergraduate course in media literacy or introduction to media studies, it still retains many of the chapters and lessons from previous editions. In this way, you can think of this book as "Media Literacy, 1st Edition," or as "Practical Media Literacy, 3rd Edition." While this book is still accessible to non-academics, it is certainly more rigorous and robust than previous editions, making it an ideal choice for an undergrad college course, or for an introductory graduate course in cultural or media studies.

The key to understanding media literacy is the ability to think critically about the information around us. As such, this book takes a broader view of media than do many other texts in this field. In this book, we analyze not only traditional as well as digital media, but also events, static icons like logos, and other observations and experience that seek to deliver a message through the basic process of communication. As such, in this text, we first take a basic approach to examine the basics of communication. What is communication? How do we communicate, as humans and as members of a group. We must first understand these concepts before we can learn to communicate through media, which is an abstraction of communication between two people or two groups. This abstraction will be the concern of the remainder of the book, but the reader will find themselves returning to these basic ideas of communication throughout the book.

One of the biggest secrets of media literacy, and of this book, is that the ideas presented here are very simple. In fact, all of media literacy, as well as the entire knowledge base on critical thinking, can be surmised in one action: people can learn to become media literate by learning to ask the right questions about the media they consume. The key here is asking the *right* questions, not just any questions. We can ask different questions about the different media we consume, but there are very simple core questions we can ask in order to learn about any given media. After we learn to continually ask basic questions about media, we can learn to ask our own questions that make sense to us.

The idea of asking questions to dig deeper for meaning is not a new concept. This concept is called the *inquiry method.* The inquiry method works because humans are naturally inquisitive. Asking questions is how we learned about the world when we were children. We somehow knew how to ask the right questions about the world around us, and these questions helped us discover everything from culture to survival skills. But in today's complex media-saturated world, the questions we need to be asking about our world are different than what we asked as kids. Although the questions we need to ask are not difficult to ask or answer, knowing which questions to ask is the hard part.

One of the most important way to grow the critical thinking muscle, per se, is to exercise that muscle whenever possible. This is especially important after just having learned how to deconstruct a media message to its basic elements. As such, each chapter contains lesson plans at the end of the chapter to practice the skills just learned. These lesson plans are meant to practice your important skills on real world media. Each lesson has been written to teach a particular aspect of media analysis, and can be assigned as homework or as in-class activities.

Acknowledgements

The creation of this book has been a journey that began long ago with a strong desire to make it easy for people to become media literate. Many of the ideas I present here were arrived at after careful consideration and research, and after discussing the ideas with colleagues and even with people not involved in education at all.

I first need to thank my wife Rosaline, who works tirelessly to keep me on course and focused on my work.

I would like to thank my colleagues, Mathew Needleman of Video In The Classroom, Marieli Rowe and Karen Ambrosh from the National Telemedia Council, Sr. Rose Pacatte of the Pauline Center for Media Studies, Jeff Share of UCLA, media literacy pioneer Elizabeth Thoman, Tessa Jolls from the Center for Media Literacy, and Frank Dawson, Nancy Grass, and Brad Lemonds from Santa Monica College, all of whom have helped guide me in my career as a media literacy educator.

I would also like to thank my mentors at Action for Media Education, including Marilyn Cohen, Linda Kennedy, and Michael Danielson.

To all of my students, who teach me more than I can ever teach them.

Introduction to the First Edition

In 1900, parents and teachers were happy teaching kids how to read books. Kids learned the letters in the alphabet and were taught that putting letters together would make words, those words strung together would make sentences, and several sentences next to each other conveyed larger meaning. In 1900, with newspapers and books being the main sources of information, learning how words and their combinations were used to convey meaning was all that kids needed to learn to interpret the world around them.

People who did not know how to read in 1900 were at an absolute disadvantage compared with people who could read. Without radio or television, and with newspapers the only source of information beyond your immediate existence, not knowing how to read meant not understanding the world, not knowing about the events changing the world, and not being able to know the information you needed to know in order to succeed. In 1900, reading was an essential and basic skill.

Fast forward to today. We now live in a world dominated by a wide variety of media types coming from an even wider variety of sources. Today, information might come from books and newspapers, but it is more likely to come from television and social media. Today we are capable of receiving the same information on a variety of devices, including mobile devices like smart phones and tablets. So today the delivery method is not as important (but still plays a part, as we will find out) as the source of the information.

People today are bombarded with information telling them to buy this or believe that. A new paradigm for creating media is being established – the Internet is near ubiquitous, technology costs are way down, and access to media creation tools is way up. This means that anyone with access to a computer can become a creator of media. At the same time, costs to produce traditional media like TV shows and newspapers are higher than ever, and these traditional media outlets experience increasing pressure to make a profit by reaching the largest audience possible. This has created an over-saturated marketplace for ideas, with too much information vying for our constant, though limited, attention.

In today's multimedia-driven world, reading and writing are not as important as they used to be. Even if you do not know how to read, today you can still get yourself from one place to the next, order food at a restaurant, be entertained by your favorite TV show or sport, and live a full life. If you do not believe me, I can give you the example of one of my former students, Daniel. Daniel is blind and cannot read – not even Braille, as he has a condition that affects the nerves in his fingers – and he still manages to achieve all of the things I mentioned above and more. Daniel is a college graduate, and he has never seen what a letter or a word or a sentence looks like. Of course, Daniel also does not know what actors or movie sets or music videos look like, but he still manages to be culturally savvy and very popular with his peers and colleagues.

Daniel is a prime example of how the media influences and informs us, even if we cannot see or read. This is because today we receive huge amounts of information through all of our senses, not just our eyes. This means that in order to be fully functional members of society, we should understand the media's impact on our lives, and we should learn how to make decisions about the media we consume. We need to understand that, just like a hamburger is a product in a restaurant, the various types of media we consume are consumption products as well. And just as we try to make healthy food choices when eating out (like skipping the fries with our hamburger), we need to learn how to make healthy media choices (like skipping certain commercials or programs altogether). And just like hamburgers are based on ingredients, and books are based on letters and words, we should understand the various elements that make up the media we consume if we want to understand its meaning – and its effects on our lives.

The earlier we learn to be critical of media, the better off we will be throughout our lives. Children too young to read can still understand the various symbols creating meaning around them. For example, young girls dressed in pink clothing begin associating themselves with those colors, especially when they start recognizing that boys are being dressed in blue. As children develop, they learn to make connections like "pink equals girl, blue equals boy." Another example of how children are impacted by symbols creating meaning around them is with the restaurant with a yellow "M" as its logo. Children do not understand the ideas behind the logo, but as soon as they learn about it they start associating the logo with the thought "yummy." These are just two simple examples of how symbols affect us, even if we cannot read and can barely understand the world. Imagine how symbols with much more complex meanings (like the hundreds of symbols and elements that make up a television commercial) affect us. This is why people should start learning the impact of these various symbols from a young age.

In 2005 I began my journey of learning about how the media affects us at the deepest level, and how it also affects society at the deepest level. Prior to 2005 I had spent nine years working in media production, mostly spent producing music, radio programming, and advertising. I was involved in creating media for regional and national clients, and for all intents and purposes, I was the media. I had studied audio and video production at the university, and I was impacting society with the work I was doing.

Before 2005, I thought of the media as this ubiquitous system that programming appeared on. Because of my own past as a producer, I knew that TV networks produced television shows and that they made money through advertising. I was also well aware that a radio station's job was to play music and keep people entertained while they were working or out driving. I knew that newspapers contained printed news stories, and that it was mostly older people that read them. And I understood that the Internet was this vast space full of information and ideas created by faceless "netizens" for my perusal and enjoyment. As a member of society I understood these things, and because of my training I was even good at creating some of it. I was a media consumer in every respect, but it was not until 2005 that I "woke up" and began understanding how media affected me deep down. Media theorist Marshall McLuhan said that the medium was the message, and despite my own training and my lifetime of experiencing media's messages, this seemed like a strange idea at the time.

In 2005 I came to a very important realization: I was a passive participant in my own media production and consumption experience.

In my lifetime I had watched countless television commercials. I knew that the point of the commercial was to sell me a product or service, and that it used a combination of writing, acting, visuals, sound effects, and music to get the right message across. However, I never understood how the commercial impacted me beyond trying to sell me something. I never realized that commercials, just like other types of media, have the power to do more than just sell me a product or service. They also have the power to influence how I dress, what I choose as a career, who my friends should be, and who I should vote for. Whether I knew it or not, all of these messages were being delivered to me in the media I was consuming, but I was mostly unaware of them.

By mid-2005 and settled in my new career path, many of my colleagues at Santa Monica College were talking about media literacy. The buzz word caught on, and on a warm autumn evening, during a conference among professors, media educators, and community leaders, I could not have guessed that a topic that meant so little to me at the time would become a major focus of my academic and professional career. What I learned that evening is that the media are powerful... more powerful than most people suspect, more powerful than even I, as a media practitioner and teacher, could ever imagine. The surface ideas may not seem important, but the underlying ideas, the ones we do not notice but that affect us nonetheless, have a huge impact on how we live our lives. Media's power on us is immense, and yet most people poorly understand that power.

That night I had a revelation, and almost instantly I decided to make media literacy the central focus of my career. I could not wait to spread the word... to my students, my colleagues, my family and friends. People began calling me "Mr. Media Literacy" as this became all I talked about. I launched a media literacy website called Understand Media, and researched and wrote dozens of articles about the media's impact on our lives. I incorporated media literacy into my fundamental curriculum. I began teaching my students to think more critically about media. I told them they could start analyzing media messages by asking a simple question: why? Not just a broad "why", but a specific "why" – why does a photograph with low lighting look scary? Why does a swelling cinematic score make you cry? Why does the newscast have only a handful of stories if there is so much going on in the world? Why does a commercial entice us to buy certain products? This line of questioning would later expand beyond a simple "why", but it was a good start.

Not only would my students learn to understand the media, but they would also learn to create responsible media. After all, if you understand what influences people, you can create media that will have positive outcomes. Like the famous movie quote goes, "With great power comes great responsibility."

As I already mentioned, I have been a heavy user of media since I was very young. I owned all of the video game systems of the 80s and 90s, and my home had several television sets in it. There are many specific media experiences that I can remember as a child – the lure of Saturday morning cartoons, singing along in the car to a popular song on the radio – but one specific memory still really sticks out today. This memory sticks out because it was probably the first time I can remember being deceived by the media.

When I was about ten years old, I remember being fascinated by a toy that you wore on your feet and that was supposed to make you jump really high. I remember seeing commercials of kids jumping six feet in the air when wearing these, and I was really excited about this. As a child, given the opportunity to jump up high – and all of the fun and perhaps even power that came with that – was truly alluring. After pleading and begging with my parents, I finally got a pair of these cleverly named Moon Shoes as a birthday gift.

Imagine my disappointment when I opened the box and took out the shoes – really just a couple of plastic circular bases with webs of rubber bands in the middle for each foot – and after stepping into the shoes, I did not jump six feet into the air. I was a bit overweight as a child, so when I put the shoes on for the very first time, I sank into them. Needless to say I barely got off the ground. Looking back on this today, I probably should have known the shoes were not going to do what they said they would do. But I was so excited at the prospect of jumping really high, and the company did such a good job of appealing to my desires, I never really stood a chance.

Today, we are all confronted with our own Moon Shoes. They come in the form of media that promise us what we desire... if only we buy that product, live that lifestyle, or vote for that politician... our life will somehow be better. The media has the power to inform us, educate us, and entertain us, but we need to be mindful of the messages we choose to accept, and therefore allow to shape our lives. Media literacy is the key to living a better life in this media-saturated world, and this book will show you how to become savvier about the media that surrounds us.

Introduction to the Second Edition

The first edition of this book has been used by teachers and students around the world, and has sold thousands of copies in various formats. The book filled a need by teachers, students, and parents for a practical guide for explaining and using media literacy. I am ecstatic to know that this book has made a difference in so many people's lives.

With each endeavor, there is always room for improvement, and this book is no exception. This second edition incorporates feedback from readers, many of whom enjoyed the first edition but wanted more. Here are some things that are new in this edition.

- A stronger focus on the learner. The first edition was heavily focused on helping teachers learn how to teach media literacy. This edition assumes the reader is the person learning about media literacy, and the examples and exercises now reflect this shift.
- Expanded descriptions of different types of media. In the first edition, the focus

was on learning about the media more generally, with the assumption that all of the techniques being explained could be used for any media. In this edition, every major type of media receives its own chapter.

Introduction to the Third Edition

2016 was a watershed year for our democracy. Not only did it see the election of an autocratic businessman as president, but it also saw the media being used as a tool of intentional deceit, disruption, and distraction. Facebook, the Russians, and an endless number of small operators either spread or helped spread misinformation through all types of media, both social and traditional, ignoring fact in favor of sensationalism and pure lies.

We are now in a new world, one filled with fake news, hacked e-mail leaks, innuendo about candidates and elected officials, denials of objective facts, and misdirection to benefit a select few who know how to influence and control the new digital media landscape. Just like television changed the 1960 presidential campaign in favor of Kennedy, who understood that looks were everything on TV, the 2008 presidential election in which Obama used social media to capture the youth vote, the 2016 presidential election went to the candidate who knew how to harness the power of the new medium and game the system.

But unlike Kennedy and Obama, Trump appealed to the country's worst fears; instead of lifting us up and give us hope for our future, he created divisions and pit American against American in a battle for supreme power.

How did we get here, and more importantly, what do we do about it now? That, in part, is what this book is about. This book aims to give an overview of all media, uncover what elements lead to each medium's construction, how to understand those elements, and how to react (or not) to any particular piece of media. In a changed world (the 2nd edition of this book was published in 2015, which seems so long ago), and it is more important than ever to stay vigilant about the messages we receive. We do this by analyzing every category of media, from social media to photography, from visual media to audio-only media, from advertising to video games. We examine as much of each media, and offer lesson plans and exercises to practice these critical thinking skills. It is my belief that after you have finished this book, you will be prepared to analyze and evaluate any piece of media out in the world, including from media types that do not yet exist.

The world before Trump

You may think that the techniques associated with Trump and his administration, meant to deceive and distract, started being used in 2016, but you would be mistaken. These techniques, especially techniques used to get our attention online, have been used for as long as social media has existed, and in fact much longer than that. For as long as information has been posted online, individuals and organizations of all types have been using sketchy techniques for getting our attention, misdirecting us, and getting us to take some action.

Every media message, in fact, no matter whether it is online or in real life, has one of two goals: to sell us something, or to convince us of a point of view. In the days before the internet, television viewers, radio listeners, and newspaper readers were considered *the product* to be delivered to the *customer* (also known as *the advertiser*). Think about that for a second. You are not the customer for a television station; you do not exchange money with them in exchange for television services. You are the product the customer is buying; advertisers exchange money with the station in order to place a media message in front of you. Their hope is that you will go out and buy the product or service, or you will believe in some ideology or vote for a particular politician or political party.

Consider government propaganda. The government aims to control sentiment about different issues, and so they have teams of media specialists whose sole job is to propagate messages supporting current initiatives, while creating the illusion that the information matches the audience's values. An example is the government working with movie studios to produce movies that are pro-war or pro-capitalism. They might mix their messages with patriotic themes, helping us associate war with patriotism. In this case, the media is trying to convince us of a point of view. The movie serves as the medium by which the message is delivered.

The commercial mass media of yesteryear operated in an arena in which *gatekeepers* allowed the rich and powerful to curate the messages being delivered to the population. For example, up until the 1980s, there were only three main broadcast networks where people turned to for their television news. In order to afford having a national presence, the networks had to deliver a broad audience to advertisers. Thus, although the networks did differ in their news coverage to some degree, the requirement of reaching a large audience meant presenting information with a centrist mass appeal. Networks could not veer too left or too right on the political spectrum for fear of alienating audiences and therefore losing advertisers. This meant the diversity of voices suffered in such an environment.

There was a similar situation with printed news. While online journalism did exist by the mid-90s, even then people would only trust online versions of their local paper or a national *newspaper of record*, such as the New York Times or the Wall Street Journal. The gatekeepers had a smaller audience than television networks, and with larger cities having multiple newspapers, there was an opportunity for diversity of ideas. But still, these newspapers were still beholden to shareholders and upper management, so they still needed to deliver a large enough audience to their advertisers, which meant that the printed news must still have been mainstream and inoffensive.

In both network television as well as in print journalism, the need for large, diverse audiences meant that smaller voices were left out of the conversation. No regular citizen could wake up one day and decide to write an article or present a special report on television. The most any regular citizen could hope to achieve would be to write an op-ed and hope the editor does not believe it to be too divisive, and publishes it in a section of the newspaper generally considered to be hidden and out of the way.

The world has been plagued with media misinformation for as long as there have been media. Questioning the media has always been important. Media literacy has existed in different forms over the centuries, even before the term was ever coined. The world is just now catching up to its importance. Even before 2016, the public has been plagued with an unfair, yet powerful, media industry.

In today's interconnected world, we are bombarded with even more information and less time to digest it all before new information comes our way. We have no time, and we often lack the skillset to make sense of it all. But understanding continually-refreshing information is key to understanding our world, and making the most of it.

My sincere hope is that this book will help you understand the modern media landscape, and recognize the good and separate it from the bad. I sometimes make judgements about what is good and what is bad, but only in the most general sense. This book will teach you to analyze media and decide for yourself what is good and bad, what is deceptive and what is truthful. Unfortunately, we cannot separate the analysis of media in today's world without mentioning President Trump and his use of media, so he and his techniques are discussed throughout, but especially in the newer sections towards the end of the book, as well as in the chapter about news and the one on social media.

Part 1 – Beginning To Understand Media Literacy

The goal of this book is to help everyday people better understand how the media impacts their lives. By deciding to read this book, you have taken the first step in the process of becoming more media literate. However, before jumping into the pond of media literacy, let us first get our feet wet by starting at the very beginning.

To start us off, we must examine the act of communication without abstractions, and we must understand how we communicate, as humans and as members of different groups. In Chapter **0** we examine the academic work of many scholars who have studied the subject, including Marshall McLuhan, Audre Lorde, and Stuart Hall.

Before we can learn about media literacy, we first need to understand the fundamental idea of "what is media?" Where does the word *media* come from, and how do we define what media are and what media are not. Despite our preconceived notions about the media, media can be different things to different people – it can be broad or narrow. This is why it is so important to define the concept of media as we will use it in this book. We learn about the definition of media in Chapter **1**.

After we learn about the concept of media, next we need to learn a definition for media literacy. Although countless academics have come up with theories about what media literacy is all about, you would be surprised at what a simple concept it really is. We also need to understand the components within media literacy. We begin to really understand the concepts and ideas behind media literacy in Chapter **2**.

If media literacy is so important, why is not everyone learning media literacy – in school, at universities, through adult education programs? Why is media literacy not considered a basic skill like English and math? These are great questions with sometimes complex answers. In Chapter **3**, we try to examine the problems involved in bringing media literacy to the classroom and how to address these issues.

In Chapter **4** we will discuss a new way of looking at media literacy – as a practical application instead of as a collection of academic theories. Media literacy is a practical skill that everyone should have, and so teaching it and learning it should be easy and simple. Making media literacy accessible to as many people as possible increases its power, and helps give power to those who learn how to use it. That is what this entire book is about!

Hopefully by the end of this book you will have enough knowledge about media literacy and its concepts to use it in a practical way in your life. You will know enough to recognize when the media are shaping your thinking, and you will know techniques needed to think critically about the media's messages. You will also have enough knowledge to teach the basics of media literacy to others. Use the activities in **Part 2** to refine your own media literacy skills, and teach media literacy to other people.

One thing to know is that being media literate is not like turning a light switch on or off. Being media literate is more like learning any other skill in life – you start with some basic understanding, and then you become better at it with time. If you are reading this book, you are already aware that the media influences you, so you are already media literate! The goal is to become better at understanding the media, not being perfect at it. Even I still get caught up by an impressively produced movie or television commercial. We do the best that we can, and learn new lessons every day. But you need to start somewhere.

So let us get started on our journey to understand the media by understanding media literacy.

Chapter 0: Understanding Communication

In this chapter we will take our first looks at understanding how communication works, which will lead us to a greater understanding of how the media works. Much of this chapter is academic in nature, and references the work of many scholars who came before me, including Claude Shannon and Warren Weaver, Stuart Hall, and Marshall McLuhan. Most of this chapter is cited from Wikipedia, and reflects original ideas which are not my own. This chapter will serve as a foundation for later topics and exercises.

The reason this deep dive on communication is necessary is because we look at the process of communication without the abstraction layer of media. This allows us to see what is going on behind the scenes when a communication happens. This is basic communication – no camera, no microphone, no computer screen, and it can be between two humans, a human and a machine, a human and a cat or dog, etc. After we understand these basics, we can add the abstraction layer of media on top of communication to understand how we communicate electronically through our devices. You will find the process is similar, and that what is added is noise, which could be a deterrent to understanding the message.

The Basics of Communication

Communication (from Latin *communicare*, meaning "to share") is the act of conveying meanings from one entity or group to another through the use of mutually understood signs, symbols, and semiotic rules.

The main steps inherent to all communication are:

1. The formation of communicative motivation or reason.
2. Message composition (further internal or technical elaboration on what exactly to express).
3. Message encoding (for example, into digital data, written text, speech, pictures, gestures and so on).
4. Transmission of the encoded message as a sequence of signals using a specific channel or medium.

5. Noise sources such as natural forces and in some cases human activity (both intentional and accidental) begin influencing the quality of signals propagating from the sender to one or more receivers.
6. Reception of signals and reassembling of the encoded message from a sequence of received signals.
7. Decoding of the reassembled encoded message.
8. Interpretation and making sense of the presumed original message.

Below is the Shannon and Weaver model of communication, which includes feedback from the receiver.

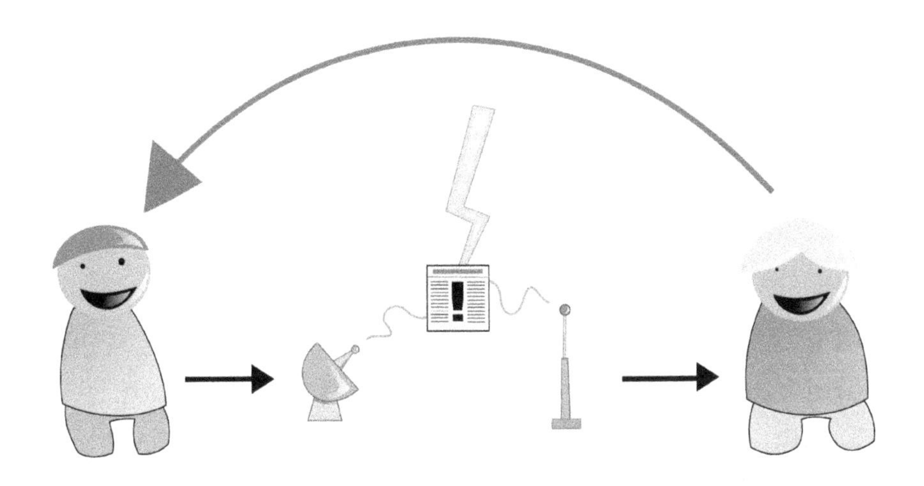

Figure 1: By Einar Faanes - Own work, CC BY-SA 3.0, https://commons.wikimedia.org/w/index.php?curid=620293

Information for this section sourced from Wikipedia: https://en.wikipedia.org/wiki/Communication

The Meaning of the Message

Stuart Hall

Stuart Hall is a cultural theorist and sociologist who has lived and worked in the United Kingdom since 1951. Hall's work covers issues of hegemony and cultural studies, taking a post-Gramscian stance. He regards language-use as operating within a framework of power, institutions and politics/economics. This view presents people as producers and consumers of culture at the same time. (Hegemony, in Gramscian theory, refers to the cultural production of "consent" as opposed to "coercion".)

For Hall, culture is not something to simply appreciate or study, but a "critical site of social action and intervention, where power relations are both established and potentially unsettled."

Hall has become one of the main proponents of reception theory, and developed Hall's Theory of encoding and decoding. This approach to textual analysis focuses on the scope for negotiation and opposition on the part of the audience. This means that the audience does not simply passively accept a text — social control.

Encoding and Decoding

Hall presented his encoding and decoding philosophy in various publications and at a several oral events across his career. The first was in "Encoding and Decoding in the Television Discourse" (1973), a paper Hall wrote for the Council of Europe Colloquy on 'Training In The Critical Readings of Television Language' organized by the Council & the Centre for Mass Communication Research at the University of Leicester.

Hall takes a semiotic approach and builds on the work of Roland Barthes and Umberto Eco. The essay takes up and challenges long held assumptions on how media messages are produced, circulated and consumed, proposing a new theory of communication. "The 'object' of production practices and structures in television is the production of a message: that is, a sign-vehicle or rather sign-vehicles of a specific kind organized, like any other form of communication or language, through the operation of codes, within the syntagmatic chains of a discourse".

"Before this message can have an 'effect' (however defined), or satisfy a 'need' or be put to a 'use', it must first be perceived as a meaningful discourse and meaningfully de-coded".

Hall identifies three main codes or positions. The first is the dominant or hegemonic code. It is the code the encoder expects the decoder to recognize/decode. "When the viewer takes the connoted meaning from, say, a television newscast or current affairs program, full and straight, and decodes the message in terms of the reference-code in which it has been coded, we might say that the viewer is operating inside the dominant code".

The second is the professional code. It operates in tandem with the dominant code. "It serves to reproduce the dominant definitions precisely by bracketing the hegemonic quality, and operating with professional codings which relate to such questions as visual quality, news and presentational values, televisual quality, 'professionalism' etc.".

The third is the negotiated code. "It acknowledges the legitimacy of the hegemonic definitions to make the grand significations, while, at a more restricted, situational level, it makes its own ground-rules, it operates with 'exceptions' to the rule".

The final position Hall identifies is the oppositional code, also known the globally contrary code. "It is possible for a viewer for a viewer perfectly to understand both the literal and connotative inflection given to an event, but to determine to decode the message in a globally contrary way".

Hall challenged all three components of the mass communications model. It argued that (i) meaning is not simply fixed or determined by the sender; (ii) the message is never transparent; and (iii) the audience is not a passive recipient of meaning. For example, a documentary film on asylum seekers that aims to provide a sympathetic account of their plight, does not guarantee that audiences will decode it to feel sympathetic towards the asylum seekers. Despite its being realistic and recounting facts, the documentary form itself must still communicate through a sign system (the aural-visual signs of TV) that simultaneously distorts the intentions of producers and evokes contradictory feelings in the audience.

Distortion is built into the system, rather than being a "failure" of the producer or viewer. There is a "lack of fit" Hall argues "between the two sides in the communicative exchange". That is, between the moment of the production of the message ("encoding") and the moment of its reception ("decoding"). In "Encoding/decoding", Hall suggests media messages accrue a common-sense status in part through their performative nature. Through the repeated performance, staging or telling of the narrative of "9/11" (as an example; but there are others like it within the media) a culturally specific interpretation becomes not only simply plausible and universal, but is elevated to "common-sense".

Source: http://en.wikipedia.org/wiki/Stuart_Hall_(cultural_theorist)

Connotation and Denotation

Connotation and Denotation are two principal methods of describing the meanings of words.

Connotation refers to the wide array of positive and negative associations that most words naturally carry with them, whereas denotation is the precise, literal definition of a word that might be found in a dictionary.

Introduce the idea of connotation, defining it as the associations that people make with a word. You can contrast connotation with the denotative value of a word, its more literal meaning, and give an example of a word (such as "chicken"). Connotation is the emotional and imaginative association surrounding a word. Denotation is the strict dictionary meaning of a word.

Connotation and denotation are not two separate things/signs. They are two aspects/elements of a sign, and the connotative meanings of a word exist together with the denotative meanings.

- Connotation represents the various social overtones, cultural implications, or emotional meanings associated with a sign.
- Denotation represents the explicit or referential meaning of a sign. Denotation refers to the

literal meaning of a word, the 'dictionary definition.'

For example, the name 'Hollywood' connotes such things as glitz, glamour, tinsel, celebrity, and dreams of stardom. In the same time, the name 'Hollywood' denotes an area of Los Angeles, worldwide known as the center of the American movie industry.

Diction, an element of style, refers to the words writers use to express ideas. Words convey more than exact, literal meanings, in which case they "connote" or suggest additional meanings and values not expressed in general dictionary definitions. Words that "denote" a core meaning are those that are generally used and understood by the users and the audience to represent an object or class of objects, an act, a quality, or an idea. However, because of usage over time, words that denote approximately the same thing may acquire additional meanings, or connotations, that are either positive (meliorative) or negative (pejorative).

Consider the changes undergone by these words in the 20th century: liberal, diversity, team player, right wing, follower, gay, minority, feminist, left wing, abuse, conservative, motherhood, extremist, rights, relationship, harassment, family, propaganda, peacekeeper, and comrade.

drug addict . . . druggie, drug fiend, substance abuser

handicapped . . . crippled, disabled, differently abled

horse . . . . . . steed, nag, plug

house . . . . . . home, abode, domicile, residence

thin . . . . . . thin, slender, slim, skinny, lean, beanpole

attractive . . . pretty, beautiful, handsome, fair

reporter . . . . journalist, broadcaster, newshound

unattractive . . plain, dull, ugly

- The media were swarming around the pileup on the innerbelt to capture every conceivable injury for the evening news.
- The journalists were on the scene at the innerbelt crash to document the incident for the evening news.
- Photographers stood patiently along the walkway, awaiting the arrival of the Oscar nominees.

- The paparazzi lined the walkway anxiously poised to snap the Oscar nominees.
- America's Midwest is often referred to as the heartland by Washington congressmen.
- America's Midwest is often referred to as flyover country by DC politicos.

Words have both **denotations** (literal meanings) and **connotations** (suggestive meanings). Fungus is a scientific term denoting a certain kind of natural growth, but the word also has certain connotations of disease and ugliness.

Connotations can be both positive and negative; for example, lady carries a hint of both elegance and subservience. The influence of connotative meaning can also change the denotative meaning, one example being the thoroughly transformed word "gay".

- Denotation refers to the literal meaning of a word, the "dictionary definition."" For example, if you look up the word snake in a dictionary, you will discover that one of its denotative meanings is "any of numerous scaly, legless, sometimes venomous reptiles having a long, tapering, cylindrical body and found in most tropical and temperate regions."

- Connotation, on the other hand, refers to the associations that are connected to a certain word or the emotional suggestions related to that word. The connotative meanings of a word exist together with the denotative meanings. The connotations for the word snake could include evil or danger.

https://en.wikipedia.org/wiki/Stuart_Hall_(cultural_theorist)#Encoding_and_decoding_model

The Medium is the Message

Marshall McLuhan

Herbert Marshall McLuhan was a Canadian philosopher, whose work is among the cornerstones of the study of media theory. Born in Edmonton, Alberta, McLuhan studied at the University of Manitoba and the University of Cambridge. He began his teaching career as a professor of English at several universities in the US and Canada before moving to the University of Toronto in 1946, where he remained for the rest of his life.

McLuhan coined the expression "the medium is the message" and the term global village, as well as predicting the World Wide Web almost 30 years before it was invented. He was a fixture in media discourse in the late 1960s, though his influence began to wane in the early 1970s. In the years following his death, he continued to be a controversial figure in academic circles. However, with the arrival of the Internet and the World Wide Web, interest would be renewed in his work and perspective.

Understanding Media (1964)

McLuhan's most widely-known work, Understanding Media: The Extensions of Man (1964), is a seminal study in media theory. Dismayed by the way in which people approach and use new media such as television, McLuhan famously argues that in the modern world "we live mythically and integrally...but continue to think in the old, fragmented space and time patterns of the pre-electric age."

McLuhan proposed that media themselves, not the content they carry, should be the focus of study—popularly quoted as "the medium is the message." McLuhan's insight was that a medium affects the society in which it plays a role not by the content delivered over the medium, but by the characteristics of the medium itself. McLuhan pointed to the light bulb as a clear demonstration of this concept. A light bulb does not have content in the way that a newspaper has articles or a television has programs, yet it is a medium that has a social effect; that is, a light bulb enables people to create spaces during nighttime that would otherwise be enveloped by darkness. He describes the light bulb as a medium without any content. McLuhan states that "a light bulb creates an environment by its mere presence." More controversially, he postulated that content had little effect on society—in other words, it did not matter if television broadcasts children's shows or violent programming, to illustrate one example—the effect of television on society would be identical. He noted that all media have characteristics that engage the viewer in different ways; for instance, a passage in a book could be reread at will, but a movie had to be screened again in its entirety to study any individual part of it.

"Hot" and "Cool" Media

In the first part of Understanding Media, McLuhan states that different media invite different degrees of participation on the part of a person who chooses to consume a medium. A cool medium incorporates increased involvement but decreased description, while a hot medium is the opposite, decreasing involvement and increasing description. In other words, a society that appears to be actively participating in the streaming of content but not considering the effects of the tool is not allowing an "extension of ourselves." A movie is thus said to be "high definition," demanding a viewer's attention, while a comic book to be "low definition," requiring much more conscious participation by the reader to extract value. "Any hot medium allows of less participation than a cool one, as a lecture makes for less participation than a seminar, and a book for less than a dialogue."

Some media, such as movies, are hot—that is, they enhance one single sense, in this case vision, in such a manner that a person does not need to exert much effort in filling in the details of a movie image. Hot media usually, but not always, provide complete involvement without considerable stimulus. For example, print occupies visual space, uses visual senses, but can immerse its reader. Hot media favor analytical precision, quantitative analysis and sequential ordering, as they are usually sequential, linear, and logical. They emphasize one sense (for example, of sight or sound) over the others. For this reason, along with film, hot media also include radio, the lecture, and photography.

McLuhan contrasts hot media with cool—specifically, television, which he claims requires more effort on the part of the viewer to determine meaning; and comics, which, due to their minimal presentation of visual detail, require a high degree of effort to fill in details that the cartoonist may have intended to portray. Cool media are usually, but not always, those that provide little involvement with substantial stimulus. They require more active participation on the part of the user, including the perception of abstract patterning and simultaneous comprehension of all parts. Therefore, in addition to television, cool media include the seminar and cartoons. McLuhan describes the term cool media as emerging from jazz and popular music used, in this context, to mean "detached."

This section sourced from Wikipedia:

https://en.wikipedia.org/wiki/Marshall_McLuhan#Understanding_Media_(1964)

Audre Lorde was an American writer, feminist, womanist, librarian, and civil rights activist. She was a self-described “black, lesbian, mother, warrior, poet,” who dedicated both her life and her creative talent to confronting and addressing injustices of racism, sexism, classism, heterosexism, and homophobia. (Wikipedia)

Her writings are based on the "theory of difference," the idea that the binary opposition between men and women is overly simplistic; although feminists have found it necessary to present the illusion of a solid, unified whole, the category of women itself is full of subdivisions.

Lorde identified issues of race, class, age and ageism, sex and sexuality and, later in her life, chronic illness and disability; the latter becoming more prominent in her later years as she lived with cancer. She wrote of all of these factors as fundamental to her experience of being a woman. She argued that, although differences in gender have received all the focus, it is essential that these other differences are also recognized and addressed. "Lorde," writes the critic

Carmen Birkle, "puts her emphasis on the authenticity of experience. She wants her difference acknowledged but not judged; she does not want to be subsumed into the one general category of 'woman.'" This theory is today known as intersectionality. (Wikipedia)

This is an important concept in media as many of the images and portrayals we observe in media are “flat characters,” lacking any depth due to time or space limitations, or a disassociation with the audience. This lack of realistic representation of characters (which include characterizations of real people, for example, in the news) goes far back to the beginning of media. It used to be common in Hollywood productions, for example, to have characters on television or film be played by straight white actors, unless there was a specific reason for a character to be a different race. Throughout the 70s and 80s, television dramas often portrayed criminals as Latino or African American.

Today’s media is thankfully more diverse, and casting directors and show producers often choose diversity in their cast to have more proportionate representation. A show does not need to be about the gay community in order to portray gay characters. Women are represented more and more in leadership positions, not just to be "politically correct," but to be more representational of real life where women do hold more power in corporations than they had fifty years ago. This representation allows for more observations and examinations of intersectionality, where stories can be more relatable when they are more like real life (ex. What if the police chief is black and gay? How does that enhance the depth of the story telling and create new opportunities for exploration?)

(https://en.wikipedia.org/wiki/Audre_Lorde)

Chapter 1: What Is Media?

To understand what the media are exactly, it is first important to define the term "media." Even more specifically, we want to know about the term "mass media." Although many different meanings and interpretations may exist for the term "mass media," for our purposes we can say that the mass media *are a group of entities that construct messages with embedded values, and that disseminate those messages to a specific portion of the public in order to achieve a specific goal.*

Let us analyze this definition.

"*A group*" – When referring to the mass media as a "group," it is to say that newspapers, movie studios, television networks, radio stations, book publishers, internet websites, and so called "media conglomerates" are all a part of this group of people and companies related to the collective we call "the media."

Obviously, this group has evolved over the years. In the beginning of civilization, we only had the ability to transmit messages from person to person through words in the form of live stories and conversation. Later, humans developed written imagery and language, and messages were recorded on some sort of surface for others to consume at a later time. This was the inception of media – these surfaces with graphic or written content conveyed messages without the necessary physical presence of the author but rather through a written *medium.* This method further evolved with the ability to copy written messages over and over again. In the twentieth century we began using electronic media. At first, radio was the electronic medium of choice. This later evolved into film, then television, and eventually into the Internet.

But the definition of "a group" goes beyond what we traditionally think of as media. Besides television and movies, there are things in the world that we can include in this group. For our purposes, the group that we consider the media can be anyone or anything with a message that they deliver via some medium, such as writing or visuals. To us, this group can be a company with a brand, a political organization, or even an individual intentionally or unintentionally sending a message. This could be a friend on Facebook posting something to their wall, another friend who always wears clothing with famous logos, or even your teacher giving a lecture to your class. We are looking at the broader definition of media, because there is more in our lives besides traditional media (music and news as two examples) that influences us.

"*that constructs messages with embedded values*" – People and companies that comprise the media do not only construct messages, but also construct messages with embedded values. As we will soon discover, it is impossible to find any message in the media (or with people we know personally, for that matter) that does not contain a subjective bias. No part of the media are objective and unbiased, including the news media.

This part of the definition carries important information. If we know that all media messages have embedded values, this should immediately be a reason to analyze the media and think critically about the message before accepting it. What if the embedded values in the media message do not match your own values? This is where problems of controversy arise.

Notice that the word "constructs" was used instead of a word like "creates" or "produces." The notion that media messages are constructed means that one or more persons made a conscious effort to build the message you are viewing, listening to, or reading. The process is not dissimilar from the process of constructing a building – you need a land owner intent on building something specific, architects to create a plan, and technicians to build it. This is the same with media. For example, a magazine wants an alluring cover photo that will get people to buy the current issue, so the photographer uses specific techniques to make her subject more emotionally engaging to the viewer.

"*and that disseminates those messages*" – In order for the media to be considered a part of the group we call "the media", and not someone's own personal journal that no one else reads, the constructed messages must be disseminated – the messages must be put out into the world. In other words, the messages created by journalists, television writers, film directors, and even musical artists must be put into society for consumption in order to be considered media.

This part of the definition does not limit media by the number of people able to view the disseminated message. For example, a large newspaper with a circulation of one million copies each day is as much a part of the mass media as a person who writes an internet blog with only five people reading it, or someone posting a message on their Facebook wall for their friends to see. All these methods use their intended medium to disseminate the message into society.

Soon we will learn about the economic pressures that affect commercial media outlets. For example, running a television network is not cheap, so the owners are under pressure to deliver their media product to as many people as possible. How do you think this affects the shows that air on that network? Obviously, the network will try to make shows that appeal to the most people and will keep them watching for as long as possible. This leads to the creation of shows that are meant to appeal to, but not necessarily challenge, our existing world views.

"*to a specific portion of the public*" – Since we know that media messages are constructed, and that they all have embedded values, it is also important to know that the people and companies constructing these messages target them to a specific part of the public. The most obvious example is a local newspaper. If you live in Wichita, Kansas, it is very unlikely that you will be interested in news happening in Boulder, Colorado. Due to the proximity, the people and companies creating those messages know they should target the people most interested in reading their messages.

Proximity is only one method the media uses to target and segment its audience. As we will see later on, the media also segments its audiences based on ethnicity, nationality, religious beliefs, political beliefs, gender, class, and almost any other sub-category you can think of. There are very specific reasons that media creators do this. Mainly it is to use the media (a television program as an example) to align you and your interests with the interests of advertisers, who also group their audiences using the same categories that media creators do.

An example of this extreme grouping (media pros call it "segmentation") is in the world of magazines. The reason thousands of magazines are available for purchase is because magazine publishers know there is a target market for each magazine. A target market is the specific portion of the public likely to be interested in the message being presented, hence this portion of the definition. Take women's magazines as an example. There are literally dozens of magazines in the United States that target women. What sets the magazines apart is that they each target specific types of women. One magazine may target single, high-income women who like clothing from Europe, while another magazine might target middle class women with a family living in a dual income household.

Magazine publishers try to create a unique product meant to appeal to a specific group of people, since it would be very expensive and competitive (and ideologically impossible) to try to appeal to everyone. In fact, even a show like *American Idol* does not appeal to all of America – just a small segment of Americans who like watching singing competitions on television. That is obviously not everyone!

"*in order to achieve a specific goal*" – This last part of the definition is perhaps the most important of all. The media constructs a message, disseminates it into society, and targets specific people in order to achieve an end result. The end result is to sell you something: either a product or service, or an ideology or lifestyle.

As we will soon discover, the media have the power to convince us to believe certain things. Some of these things can be useful, for example how people are supposed to behave in society, and what values we should believe are true – American super hero movies do a great job of showing audiences who America considers to be "the good guy," and who is "the bad guy." These movies are very clear about what behaviors are acceptable in America, and what behaviors are disliked. To some degree, these behaviors reflect society – meaning they are (or should be) true, like helping someone worse off than you or being honest with people. But to some degree, these behaviors are not true, but the movie's screenwriter would hope is true – for example, the idea that violence should be used to win.

Some of the ideas that come to use from media can actually be harmful, like "blue means boy," and "pink means girl." Stereotypes, and particularly gender stereotypes, have a damaging effect on gender equality in general. Many of the disparities that exist between the genders can be traced back to parents teaching their male and female children differently.

This is where media literacy will be helpful in figuring out what is useful and what is harmful. Once we are able to recognize the distinction between the two, we will be better prepared to recognize each when they happen, and we will be able to decide for ourselves what is useful and what is harmful, since there is sometimes a very thin line that separates the two.

As with everything in life, the ideas that the media brings us and tries to convince us about are not always as subtle as blue verses pink. An extreme example of ideology in media is propaganda. This form of idea in the media is what we might consider a "hard sell," or an attempt to be over the top in order to scare us into believing the message. Political advertising is a common place for propaganda – everything from an election mailing saying to "vote for Bill or your neighborhood will not be safe," to president saying we should attack some other country because we are in danger. Even though propaganda is often direct and to the point, there are subtle messages that come from it, such as in this propaganda poster from World War 2.

Don't Let That Shadow Touch Them
Buy WAR BONDS

Media Are a Business

As we will soon discover, the media are a business selling a product (the message), to a set of consumers (the audience).

To illustrate this fact, I like to compare the media to a fast food chain, let us call it Clown's Burgers & Shakes. As a hungry consumer who does not want to cook at home, you visit Clown's, where they will make your favorite foods for you at a low price. You usually order your favorite burger with certain ingredients and not others. Clown's is happy to customize your burger to some degree, but their main ingredients, including their "secret sauce," are always included. The great thing about Clown's Burgers & Shakes is that do not sell those foods you do not like. They keep their menu simple so that is easy, convenient, and it always keeps you coming back. Just recently, a new Taco Gong opened across the street. Their Mexican / Chinese fusion dishes have become very popular lately. Clown's tried adding Tacos to their menu, but they got rid of them after a month because people were not buying them. Clown's knew what people wanted, the tried and true menu that makes peOple comfortable and does not challenge their taste buds too much. Clown's knows what customers want, and they are happy to give it to them.

If you have not caught on, Clown's Burgers and Shakes is like your typical media outlet – let us use Netflix for this example. Netflix needs to make money, and they do this by selling subscriptions to their service. In this way, Netflix is like Clown's, and you are the customer who is consuming the TV shows and movies on the service. Just like Clown's makes more money the more customers eat at their restaurants, Netflix makes more money the more people they can get to watch their shows and movies – more selection and better quality means more subscribers. This means that sometimes they may try new things – just like Clown's tried adding tacos to the menu, Netflix might try adding a new show or movie, or they might remove a popular show from their service. But if people do not watch that new show or it somehow changes the way people feel about Netflix they might remove the bad show and try to bring back the popular show that people really like. So in a way, the media are constantly trying to sell us something so that we will continue to be customers. They give us what we want, they do not try to challenge us too much, and the more we like what they give us, the more likely we are to be regular customers.

Another example of the media sells to us, is in a more direct way – through advertising. Those Facebook ads or Hulu commercials have the intention of selling you a product or service. Sometimes the ads and the content are working together to sell us a product. How many times have you seen an ad for some new car or company, and then you see that same car or company's product in the show itself. The advertisers (who help subsidize the cost of a lot of the media we consume) often have a deal with the people making the show or movie to place that product for you to see. If you favorite character is seen driving that shiny new car as she saves the world, the advertisers hope that you are more likely to buy that car because you make a positive connection between the hero and her car.

Understanding that media are a business is key to understanding the way it works. Media outlets need a high number of audience members to justify the cost of advertising to those advertisers who pay the bills. Because of the costs associated with producing content and making it available for your consumption, there is really no alternative to this situation. Even non-profit media outlets like public radio and TV stations need money to operate, and the bigger their audience, the more people will donate to help keep the station running.

It is also key to understand that advertising is the main way most media companies make money. Advertising means that the company makes money and you do not have to pay to watch your favorite show (or you pay a significant amount less than you would otherwise). This is a simple case of economics. Facebook has over a billion users, and it makes money by selling advertising slots to companies and then showing those ads to you. How many users do you think Facebook would have if they charged even $1? Most likely they would not have nearly as much as they do now. Facebook costs more to operate than the $1 it would charge customers, so it would likely need to charge more, meaning even fewer users on the site. Facebook's main idea is that it is a place where friends can connect, so they value having more users than having paid users. So instead of charging money for access, they show you advertising instead. This is the tradeoff of having advertising in media.

Of course there are other ways media companies make money, like charging monthly subscriptions or selling event tickets and merchandise. But advertising is by far the most popular way for media companies to make money, so it is worth understanding this relationship, which we will explore later on.

Are Media Real Life?

In the famous viral YouTube video, *David After Dentist*, a young boy is videotaped by his parents after he had been given sedatives during a dental visit. At one point during the video, David, confused and still in a haze, asks, "is this real life?" clearly unaware of whether what he is experiencing is real life, a dream, or maybe something else. Whether you find the video funny, sad, exploitative, or otherwise, it serves as an interesting way to frame the idea of media as it relates to the real world.

One of the vital questions we can ask about media, and which will help us better understand the ways in which the media affects us, is to understand if, and how, the media we experience reflects real life, is real life, is trying to imitate real life, or is something else. To better understand this concept, let us look at various types of media, and learn how they depict life and the world around us.

TV Shows (especially reality TV)

Reality television shows appear to depict real life and real situations, at least that is what it seems. Take a show like *Jersey Shore*, the once popular MTV reality show about a group of young people and their lives in New Jersey's Jersey Shore. The show depicted life in the Jersey Shore in a particular way, but is it real life? A bit of research on the internet would uncover some behind the scenes of the show. Not only are the people on the show told to do certain things, but the show's producers actually stage the events on the show, and have the "characters" repeat certain scenes, just to increase the drama or to direct them to a certain outcome. In other words, most of the show is staged. So is Jersey Shore real life? Does it reflect the experiences you have in your life, or are the people on the show similar to people in your own life? Or is the show a fantasy, almost like a "hyper reality" in which the events in life are super charged and exaggerated for the sake of entertainment? Even reality shows like *Deadliest Catch*, a show about fisherman who brave the cold open ocean to catch sought after seafood, is shot and edited together to be more exciting than real life. The producers edit out all of the boring parts (probably about 99% of the footage) and only keep the exciting parts. Then they add music and cut together the footage for maximum excitement.

Movies

Are movies like real life? In many ways, it would make sense that movies depict or reflect real life. Movies show people in various situations, and they look real. But as we know, movies are written by screenwriters, the characters are played by actors, and the stories follow formulas that rarely reflect the way things happen in real life. In movies, there is always a beginning, middle, and end of the story. We know that is not how life works. In real life, the world continues after issues are resolved, if issues are resolved at all. Real people do not follow a script, and we never live our lives as determined by a formula.

What about documentaries? Do documentary films depict or reflect real life? It would seem that movies that claim to document the real world would be reflective of the real world. However, these films are also constructed using editing techniques in order to tell a story. Take as an example the documentary, *Mitt*, about Mitt Romney's 2012 run for president. The film takes place over a few years, from the moment that Mitt Romney decides to run for president, to the moment he returns home after the failed campaign. It is obvious from the film that Mitt was not directed by the person shooting the video, however it is also obvious that the producer intended to show only the most interesting moments of the campaign, and with a strong desire to show Mitt in a very endearing light. The way in which the story is edited together may show real events happening, but we would also say that the film does not depict real life exactly as it happened. This is true for all documentary films, since the goal is to tell a story in under two hours using dozens, hundreds, or even thousands of hours of footage.

Music (and music videos)

Does music depict or reflect reality? Typically, songs attempt to tell a story or express an emotion in under five minutes. Often these songs are about relationships or events in life, but are they real life? Watching music videos, we see the stories played out on the screen. Similar to movies, music and music videos use formulas to tell their story. The lead singer or band convey meaning through their lyrics, the genre of music, the situation being depicted, and even through the clothing they wear. Music influences culture because it conveys a certain lifestyle or view of the world. Take the music and music videos of Jay-Z as an example. The themes in his music convey the lifestyle of a successful rap artist – nice cars, playing cards with famous people, owning lots of property, and having lots of women by your side. Is this real life, at least for most people? No, it is not, but many young people who listen to Jay-Z's music may aspire to this lifestyle, so that is one reason is can be appealing. I would guess that this is not really reflective of Jay-Z's daily life either, but it is a part of the image he conveys of himself to the world, and act, if you will. In effect, he plays a character when he is in public, while likely not being so exuberant in his private life.

Today's commercial music industry is about selling a lifestyle. We need to remember that our favorite musicians are performers that put on shows, complete with costumes and make up. To see an example of this, watch a music awards show like the Grammy's, and take a look at how many musicians in the audience are dressed in over-the-top costumes that would only be allowed as evening-wear at a music awards show. Just look at the talented, multi-Grammy-winning artist Pharrell William's clothing at the 2014 Grammy awards; in keeping with his character, he wore jeans, a red track jacket, and an over-the-top hat that would have kept him out of most any fine-dining establishment. But his persona is what makes him appealing to his fans, and so a tuxedo would be unacceptable in this case.

The News

Is the news a reflection or a depiction of real life? We would hope that this system of bringing us the latest information we care about would be real life, but even news can be said to be a distortion of real life, at best. As we will find out later in this book, the news we receive in newspapers, on TV, and through Facebook and Twitter, is all constructed and chosen for us by someone else.

Suppose an event happens in the world. The way it gets reported to us depends on several factors; who is there to experience it, how the eye witnesses tell the story, how the event is photographed or videotaped, and to whom the reporters choose to tell the story, all affect how the story of the event is told in the news. This means that, unless you were there to experience the event in person with your own senses, you will never know the full story, and even then our brains distort events over time. So is news real life? Just as with the other types of media we have discussed, it has elements of real life, but is not real life.

Social Media

When your friend posts a status update to Facebook, is this post real life? This is probably as close to real life as any of the types of media we have discussed, since we have more context – we might know more about a situation than what the friend posts on Facebook, so we can "read between the lines" – but even Facebook posts are not fully real life.

An often-repeated idea in research and in the media is that people only post things to social media that convey a particular message about themselves. Maybe a friend is sad and needs attention or sympathy, so they will post about the bad day they had. Or maybe another friend is making an announcement about something great in their lives – They are getting married, having a baby, or getting their book published – then they will post to Facebook to receive congratulations, In other words, our friends intuitively post edited information to social media just like other types of media do the same. We do not share our whole lives on social media, just the parts we actually *want* others to see. So with this, we can say that social media are not entirely real life, if at all (exaggerations and white lies are easy to conceal on Facebook).

Media reality vs. "real" reality

By simply asking the question, "are media real life," we are acknowledging the fact that the media contains, at least to some degree, depictions of real life. When we watch a movie, we know that the movie stars actors who are real people (for live-action movies), shot in real locations, and involved in situations most of us can relate to. On the news, we expect the stories being reported on to have occurred somewhere in the world.

But let us consider situations in the media that make us question the distinction between *media reality* and *real reality*. Here is a real life example that will make the point extremely clear. I follow a local cat rescue non-profit on Facebook, and they post stories and photos of cats on a regular basis. I enjoy reading these stories and looking at the pictures of cats needing a good home. The stories typically make me smile, mainly because I understand the joy of having cats myself. One day, the rescue posted a photo and story of a two-week old kitten having trouble feeding from its mother. There was an overwhelming response from the followers of the page, with people sending prayers and good thoughts for the kitten's recovery. The next day, I visited the rescue's Facebook page to see if there were any updates about the kitten. They *had* posted an update – the kitten did not make it. A huge sadness came over me, and I may have even shed a tear.

Why did this kitten's story of struggle affect me so much? I had never met the kitten, I would have never known about it without reading the Facebook post, and yet it affected me. To have such an emotional response to a photo and a story shows how media has the power to influence our thoughts, emotions, actions, and many other aspects of our lives. Just think about how this story made *you* feel. Were you sad for the kitten, just by reading the story? That is the power of media. When the world mourns the loss of a celebrity or a famous world leader, the same effect is taking place.

But the real life stories we experience through the media are not the only things that impact us on an emotional level. This same emotional response can come from hearing a song on the radio, the final scene of an intense movie, or from playing a video game. Media presents these experiences in such a way as to elicit an emotion – heart break over a sick kitten, nostalgia from a song from our youth, tearful joy that the two main characters in a movie still love each other, or anxiety during a game's climactic battle scene. All of these media experiences are constructed to illicit an emotion from the audience. Sometimes, our emotions could come naturally by relating to something in our own lives – I have cats, so stories of cats in trouble illicit emotions in me. And sometimes, our emotions can be manipulated for a particular purpose, like the negative stories dispersed by governments about other governments when a conflict is imminent (we call this propaganda, and we will talk more about it later).

Does Media Influence Society or the Other Way Around?

When discussing the media, it is useful to think about its influence on society. We know that media affects society in many ways – how we vote, what we buy, how we dress, and much more – but do we as audience members also influence the media at all? The answer is yes. As audience members, we have a big say in what information the media brings to us. I will give you a few examples to illustrate the point.

First, imagine that you are a big fan of People magazine. People magazine is a celebrity tabloid – They are known for publishing the latest news about celebrities and their lives. The audience for the magazine loves reading about their favorite stars, so they subscribe and look forward to reading the stories every week. People magazine influences its audience regarding what celebrities to focus on. If they have a desire to focus more on TV and movie stars rather than on music and fashion celebrities, they have the power to do that. The audience receives the news that People decides to print. However, the audience also has expectations – things they want to read about each week and which they know they can find in the pages of their favorite magazine. The audience also expects light-hearted portrayals in each issue. Now imagine for a moment that the editors of People magazine wanted to try something new, maybe to try to grow their readership. They start publishing more stories about celebrities that are not well known, maybe authors and music producers, and fewer articles about well-known movie and TV stars. And let us also assume the editors also began publishing articles accusing celebrities of bad behavior. To the loyal read of People magazine, these changes may turn them off of the magazine for the simple reason that the magazine no longer meets their expectations. In other words, People promised one thing but then delivered something else. After a while, readers might start canceling their subscriptions and look for other places to find their light-hearted celebrity news.

For another example of how we influence the media and how the media tries to meet our expectations, let us talk about one of my favorite comedians, Jim Carrey. I have been a fan of his for a long time, and have enjoyed his movies. Beginning in the 1990s, he had a string of hits due to his hilarious comedic portrayals in movies like *Ace Venture Pet Detective* and *Dumb and Dumber.* But one movie stands out in his repertoire of hits is *The Majestic.* Released in 2001, the movie did not have good reviews and lost money for the studio despite being directed by a critically acclaimed director (Frank Darabont), and of course starring a huge celebrity like Jim Carrey. The problem? The movie was a drama. Jim Carrey fans walked in expecting some elements of Jim Carrey's funny characters, but there was not much of that in the movie. An un-funny Jim Carrey and a running time of two hours and thirty two minutes (about an hour longer than most Jim Carrey movies) doomed the movie. People expected Jim Carrey to be funny on screen – notice earlier I called him a comedian, not an actor – and the audience's expectations were not met. It took Jim Carrey a few more years and a few more semi-dramatic roles to be taken seriously as more than just a funny man.

Hate Low-brow, Profane, Awful media? – Blame Yourself

Have you ever watched a TV show and called it your "guilty pleasure?" A guilty pleasure is typically something that we know is not acceptable to like, but we like it anyways. There is a lot of media that falls into this category. There are some really audacious reality shows that make you think, "it is shows like these that are destroying our society" or summer movies so bad that remind us of "how dumb we are becoming." These are phrases I have about guilty pleasure media – the summer action movies with gratuitous explosions, overt sexuality, and flat character, or the latest MTV hit reality show showing unintelligent people doing unintelligent things. But guess what? These media would not be out there for us to consume if the producers thought we did not want them. These media are created because there is a demand for them. There are many trends that have gotten us to this point – where we prefer to *binge watch* a show on Netflix instead of read an award-winning novel – but here we are.

The unfortunate situation is that we only have ourselves to blame. If we demanded more novels, more would be written. If we demanded more artistic movies and educational TV programs, more of these would be produced. By the same token, if we demanded more privacy online, Facebook and Google would not take our online selves for granted.

It is time we realize that the media are giving us what we expect, or at least what they think we expect. If we do not respond by saying "I will not be one more person watching this ridiculous show," we can start seeing changes in the media. However, achieving this is easier said than done.

Media literacy helps us think more critically about the media around us, and over time we come to appreciate a more diverse selection. Once we realize what is really being shown to us, and we realize the power we have to influence the media by turning off the TV or by clicking away from a website, the more we will be able to shape our media experiences.

Challenge Yourself with Media

Because the media tries to meet our expectations, they rarely challenge us to think outside of our little box that we have created for ourselves. They are afraid they might offend us or not meet our expectations, so they give us the same stories with disguised by using different characters and actors, the same songs thinly veiled using different singers, and the same ideas over and over again. Once we become comfortable, we do not usually like to challenge ourselves.

Think about it – how many radio presets do you have set in your car? Maybe ten or twelve. How many of those do you listen to the most? Maybe two or three. If you read the news online, how many sources do you get your news from? Usually one or two. We find something we like, then we mindlessly go back to it over and over again, even if it is not the best or the best *for* us. I urge you to challenge yourself in your media consumption. Change the channel, try a new website for news, or listen to a random playlist on Spotify. Try new things and you will discover new ideas and you will expand your worldview. This book will help you do this.

A Further Note about Target Markets

When we discuss target markets in media, we mean, as mentioned above, a specific group of people in society that the media chooses to focus on for their media message. With the example of women's magazines, the target market is women, and then this is further refined depending on the publication. Knowing this, we may ask ourselves, "do only women from a specific target market buy this magazine?" While the magazine publisher aims to please a specific group of women with their magazine, there may be others outside of the main target market that read the magazine as well. For example, a magazine aimed toward women between the ages of 25 to 45 may be read by teenagers or by seniors, or by men. There are many reasons this happens, but to avoid confusion we can differentiate between the people the magazine is aimed to and everyone else who reads it as well.

The **ideal demographic** (or *ideal target market*) is the percentage of people who consume some piece of media, and who are actually a part of the group the media company is aiming toward. For example, in the above example, around 80% of the people who read that women's magazine are women between the ages of 25 to 45, while everyone else would fall outside the ideal demographic into the other 20%. This formula works in most situations. Depending on how good the media outlet or advertiser is at doing segmentation and target marketing, this outsider percentage could certainly be higher. For example, a high-end shoe company might only advertise in magazines aimed toward people who are high earners to make sure that their advertising efforts reach the people who could afford their product. But that shoe manufacturer also knows that there may be people who read that magazine to day dream of a shoe they may one day be able to purchase but cannot afford right now. So about 90% of the people who see the ad in this case may be in the shoe manufacturer's ideal demographic, while the other 10% of people who see the ad are not.

This concept of ideal demographic helps explain a lot for media companies that know that their media product will be experienced by more than just the main people they are targeting. If you have ever watched a TV show or movie that you thought you would like but did not, you may not be in the ideal demographic for that show or movie, but instead in the 20% of people who watched because they were curious or thought it might be interesting. You were obviously not in the group of people that the show or movie was targeting.

Chapter 2: What Is Media Literacy?

Imagine a world where you receive thousands of messages each day. These messages are not only from your friends and family, but from strangers who want to sell you something. Maybe the strangers want to sell you one of their products or services, or maybe they want to sell you ideas they believe in. Imagine if these messages were hidden in plain sight, but you did not see and therefore were not aware of them.

This world is not one that needs to be imagined, but is in fact the world in which we live in. The strangers we just imagined are not strangers at all, but instead familiar faces, phrases, and logos we know and love. The strangers come in the form of advertisements, television programs, newspaper articles, and even musical lyrics.

These messages from strangers we are imagining come to us in the form of media. Media messages are all around us and impossible to avoid. Each day, we are bombarded by thousands of these messages, whether we realize it or not. They might be as obvious as a television commercial or television program, or as subtle as a bottle cap or an Internet article. In fact, even this book is considered a media message.

With so many media messages hitting us from every angle, it is important to realize that there is an intended purpose for each of them. The people responsible for the message you are viewing use creative techniques to get your attention. They make you become interested in their message, although you may not have originally paid attention to it.

This is why it is so important for us to not accept these media messages at face value, but instead to be critical of each and every one before accepting any of them. This is because, although many media messages may seem harmless, some messages may pose a threat to you individually, or to society as a whole through their embedded messages that influence people's ways of thinking and viewing the world and its people.

Media literacy gives us the skills to analyze media, and decide whether we will accept the messages being offered, or reject them.

So far in this book, we have been exploring the idea of the ability to critically analyze media before accepting the messages. This is what many would call media literacy. But what is media literacy exactly? There have been many definitions over the years, but most of the academic-type people have settled on a particular definition.

Media literacy is the ability to access, analyze, evaluate, and create media in all of its forms.

Let us explore this definition a bit more.

To have the ability to critically analyze media, we must first **access** that particular piece of media. This means we need to watch the TV show or movie we are going to analyze, not just hear someone's review about it. The access part is very important, and it could mean different things to different people. For example, people with hearing impairments cannot hear a television show, so this affects the way they interpret its message. Listening to a song in a language you do not understand will have the same effect – you will ultimately interpret the message differently than someone who accesses the song in their native language and understands its lyrics as well as subtleties of its genre.

After we access a piece of media, we can **analyze** that piece of media to begin understanding it. When we analyze a piece of media, we are thinking about the components or elements that make up that media. We try to be as objective as possible in our analysis, and we try to avoid any bias in our examination. We can take a morning television news program as an example. We might analyze the program by asking objective questions like "how many news anchors are on the program, and what do they look like?" "What are the news stories about?" "What are the commercials for during the program?" These questions will get us to start thinking about the news program so that we can begin evaluating what we discovered.

When we **evaluate** a piece of media, we try to think critically about the components and elements we discovered when we analyzed it. This is when we would use a lot of these "why" type questions. For our example of examining a television news program, we might ask "why did they choose that news anchor instead of someone from a different gender or race?" "Why do they talk a lot about local stories, but not a lot about national or international stories?" "Why are a lot of the stories about bad things that happen in the world?" "Why did they pick these particular news stories to talk about and not something else?" These questions help us evaluate the messages at a much deeper level than merely analyzing the components.

Finally, after we think we understand the message that was sent to us in the particular piece of media we examined, we want to prove we really understand it by **creating** our own media of this type. With our television news example, you might try writing and producing your own news show with a home video camera. You will know what to talk about, how to set up the camera, and how to dress because you understand these elements in the real thing. This part is often called "synthesis" by the academics, and it is an important aspect of understanding media. If when you watch your home TV news show something seems off, you will understand this inconsistency at a much deeper level because you have really studied it.

The point of following these four steps to become media literate about a particular piece of media is so you can be hyper aware of the media you experience. For example, if you perform the four steps with the television news program as suggested above, the next time you watch the morning news you will think about it differently. You will think more critically about it without having to think as hard about it. In other words, you will have internalized the techniques for analyzing this particular type of media, and your brain will do this in a more automatic fashion in the future.

When we look at the media, we often do not realize that this ever-present source of information has a powerful influence over us. Just as a fish does not realize it lives in the water, we do not realize we are exposed to these influential messages. We do not know a world without it, since we have been with it all our lives.

By and large, this has led us to become passive in the way we consume media. We take it for granted, and this can be very dangerous. Advertisers and media creators know of our passive ways, and they prey on this deficiency, creating messages with subtle hints to buy products or believe a lifestyle or ideology.

To better understand the way media affects us, and how we can become active consumers of media, we must take a look at the core concepts behind media literacy. Although we do not want to get too far into the stuffy academics of it all, it is important to at least know a bit about each of these concepts.

These concepts are adapted from ideas from the **Center for Media Literacy** and from the **National Association for Media Literacy Education**.

All media messages are "constructed."

Just as books use letters to make words, words to make sentences, sentences to make paragraphs and paragraphs to tell us a story, media sources have their own set of rules to create their messages.

When we say that all media messages are constructed, we mean that all media messages have been assembled by someone. That "someone" could be a single person, or it could be a lot of people at a large organization. The messages and values embedded in this particular piece of media are those of the people who created it.

In photographs, the photographer's own vision of what she wants to show within the frame demonstrates her own values and beliefs. A newspaper writer's articles may be based on his own beliefs, or based on the beliefs and ideologies of his publishers, or perhaps even the beliefs of the companies who advertise in that particular newspaper.

Since all media messages are constructed using the creator's own ideologies and values, media messages from different creators will have different ideas embedded in them. The ideas embedded in each piece of media come from the creators' own experiences, and since everyone's experiences are different, we can expect that each media message should be different as well.

The reason this is important is because not all media messages will have messages you agree with, since your experiences and ideologies will sometimes be different from those of the message's creators. While you may experience a certain media message in one way, there are others who will most certainly experience it in a completely different way. For example, while you may find a particular media message amusing, there may be others who find it offensive.

The media message's construction is not only based on the creator's own ideas and ideologies, but also on a pre-defined set of rules for that particular type of media. A photographer uses camera angles, lighting, and lens length to get her ideas across, while radio producers use voices, sound effects, and music to convey their ideas. Each type of media must adhere to its own set of rules in order to construct the intended message.

Each medium has different characteristics, strengths, and a unique "language" of construction.

A photograph is constructed using a different process than a book. Each medium uses unique methods for constructing its messages.

It may seem obvious to say that each medium is constructed differently, noting for example the difference in constructing the messages in a book compared to constructing the messages in a film. At its most basic level, a book requires the creator to write or type thoughts onto paper or a computer screen, while a film requires many creators to work together in creating a product that includes sound and live or animated motion.

Consider the language used in photography to describe the process of creation. Photographers use terms such as "wide shot", "close up", "deep focus", and "f-stops". Someone writing a book would probably be more concerned with "chapters", "logical flow", "character development", and "story". Each medium uses its own language or process of creation, and this process makes each medium unique.

This is not to say that language cannot be shared among various media. Convergence brings together two or more mediums to create a new one. This may seem like a new term, but consider movies, a convergence medium created through the combination of theatre and photography. In this case, movies contain language from both theatre ("staging", "actor") and photography ("close up", "film").

To some, the concept of a unique language may not seem apparent, especially when analyzing and comparing messages from the same type of media. Consider the medium of television - all messages constructed for television must be created using cameras, microphones, writers, directors, actors, etc. But television is so broad, that messages in different types of content can be constructed using their own language in the same medium.

As an example, compare the construction of a television commercial and a reality show. Both are created using the same language, but they are created for different purposes and so must be constructed differently. Another example of this is a fiction book versus a non-fiction book - both are books, created using a set of rules unique to their medium, but both hope to achieve different goals (to entertain or to inform), and both have a unique language within their specific area.

It is important to understand that each medium has different characteristics, strengths, and a unique language of construction.

Media messages are produced for particular purposes.

Every media message is meant to either sell you a product or service, or to convince you of a lifestyle or ideology. Every single one.

The third core concept of media literacy is that all media messages are produced for a particular purpose. In fact, most media outlets can be lumped into two main groups: media outlets that want to sell us a product or a service, and media outlets that want to sell us a lifestyle or ideology.

Many media outlets are commercial outlets, and their revenues are gained by selling us a product or service by giving us content we like, such as a television show or a newspaper, and then mixing in the ads so we can buy those products and services. But not all media outlets are commercial in nature. Many media outlets are of a non-commercial nature, though these outlets still intend to sell us something.

Since we are using the broader definition of media that includes people and their individual ideas, let us take for example a speech by a politician. The politician has a message he or she wants to deliver to the public, so the politician can be considered a type of media. But the politician is not trying to sell us laundry detergent or clothing. Politicians, just like other non-commercial media outlets, want to sell us on their ideas of how the world should work.

Other types of non-commercial media outlets that want to sell us their ideologies or lifestyles might be an organized religion, convincing us to believe in a particular truth about life, our families, teaching us their views on right and wrong from a young age, and even our friends, convincing us that we should go to that concert because "everyone else is going."

Commercial and non-commercial media are all around us, and both types have embedded values and ideologies in their messages, and with enough repetition, both types have the ability to sell us something. While one type of media outlet us revenue is gained through the direct sale of a product or service, the other type of media outlet us metaphoric revenue is gained through convincing us of an ideology or lifestyle.

Sometimes, the two types of sales happen simultaneously. For example, a popular youth-oriented fast food chain may try to sell their products through an advertisement during a television program that tries to sell a youthful and hip lifestyle, such as a show about music. The advertisement and television program work together to help validate each other as appropriate messages for their target market. This is why people who associate themselves with certain lifestyles are usually attracted by the same brands. The media has helped solidify the marriage between the product and the lifestyle.

All media messages contain embedded values and points of view.

The message creator has either consciously or subconsciously embedded their own values in the message.

For those wanting to be truly media literate, it is crucial to understand that all media messages contain embedded values and points of view. Further, all media messages contain at least two types of values and at least two points of view - those of the creator, and those of the audience.

To illustrate this point, consider an evening newscast on local television. Although we would like to believe that news is unbiased and free of prejudice, this is not the case. Even by a simple choice of words, such as calling someone a "victim", a "gang member", or a "suspect", prejudice is being introduced into the message.

The people who write the newscast are using their point of view to present news about the world to their audience. Media creators produce media using their own background and experiences as reference points.

Since everyone is different, everyone has a different point of view of the world.

To be free of bias, the newscasters would need to refer to each person they talk about as a "person" - "this person was arrested", "this person is in the hospital". Even then, we are showing a bias for being humans. And in this case, the news would be boring, which means it probably would not be watched by many people.

Media messages also must contain the values of their audience members in order to be accepted by them. For example, although a newspaper editor might want to expose a large local company for wrong doing (the editor's bias), he or she might not do it because it could mean many lost jobs for the readers of the newspaper. The audience would either reject the story, lowering the credibility or readership of the newspaper, or it may damage the local economy, which may in turn affect the newspaper's own business. These are decisions media creators need to make each day.

People use their individual skills, beliefs and experiences to construct their own meanings from media messages.

Each person interprets media messages based on their own backgrounds and experiences, and so each person's interpretation will be different.

Since every person has a unique background and unique experiences, each person will react differently to each message. This is not to say that we do not react similarly to certain messages, but each reaction will still be unique.

As an example, consider the popularity of certain shows on television. The television networks know that a large group of people will enjoy a particular show, but that another large group will not like it. The show's creators try to include as much content deemed appealing by a large group of society to make the show likeable, but even fans of the show will like and dislike certain aspects more than others.

Take a show like *The Voice*. Although there are millions of people watching each week, people within that fan base have differing opinions about who should win. Depending on each fan's musical tastes, geographic location, age, and gender, they will like a particular contestant more than another.

Another example is the media coverage of political candidates. Since most people do not meet directly with politicians, we receive the information about them through the media - television commercials and debates, websites, newspapers and magazines, radio addresses, etc. Since we all have different backgrounds, different needs from society, and different points of view about the direction we want society to go in, we will each pick the candidate that most matches our point of view about the world.

People use their individual skills, beliefs, and experiences to construct their own meanings from media messages.

Media and media messages can influence beliefs, attitudes, values, behaviors, and the democratic process.

Although people are influenced by their friends, family, and community leaders as well as media, media influences all of those people as well.

Many media educators enjoy discussing media effects, and for good reason. Although a single exposure to a particular message is not likely to change someone's opinion on any particular topic, continued exposure to media messages will help shape points of view over time.

As an example, a single exposure to a media message about the desire for expensive cars will not influence someone to purchase an expensive car, but experiencing multiple messages from many sources (commercials, TV shows, movies, music, newspapers) over a period of time may shape a person's opinion about expensive cars the next time they consider buying a new car.

Of course, to say the media alone is an influencing factor would be dismissing the influential power of family, friends, community leaders, and our own experiences. But imagine if our family, friends, and community leaders are shaped by the same media that shapes us, as is the case in American society. In this case, influential media messages are more easily absorbed at the subconscious level since everyone around us believes the same thing.

Ultimately, each person decides for him/herself how to view the world, but even these decisions are shaped by media's influence. Most people do not want to fall out of the mainstream (as defined on a large scale such as American society, or on a smaller scale as a member of a smaller group), and so they will make decisions that are accepted by society, a society that is influenced on a mass scale by the media.

Media and media messages can influence beliefs, attitudes, values, behaviors, and the democratic process.

Chapter 3: A Practical Approach to Learning Media Literacy

Over the years, I have spent a lot of time interacting with people who are media literacy "experts". These people are smart, intellectual, well spoken, and with lots of degrees to their credit. They do amazing research and publish important works that helps advance our understanding of media literacy. Despite all of the extensive research these scholars have contributed to the field of media literacy, many of them have limited experience of teaching media literacy principles to regular people. The result is that there seems to be a missing bridge between the academic parts of media literacy and the more practical parts.

I belong to several online media literacy communities – e-mail lists and discussion forums where people discuss media education. They also discuss current events and talk about how the media has done something right or wrong. These online communities are great resources – if you are an academic. But very little of this information is useful if you are trying to actually learn media literacy skills or to teach media literacy to a room full of students.

You see, media literacy is not just an academic subject. Its primary purpose is not to be a topic of debate among graduate students and university professors. Its primary purpose is to help people better appreciate the media's influence on us, and to think critically about the media we consume. It is meant to enlighten us and to teach us to be active when watching TV or reading a newspaper.

This is not to say that media literacy ideas cannot originate from academia, because they can and they have. People of great resources and intelligence have pondered long and hard about what media are, and what it means to truly understand them – I am proud to call these people my colleagues. But in the end, it is what we do with the information that truly defines media literacy.

Media literacy is a life skill. What students learn about it in the classroom will hopefully be carried with them throughout their lives. The skills learned in media education can be applied to any area in life. Students who learn media literacy tend to become more efficient critical thinkers in general.

Because we are all media consumers, it is worth taking a few moments to talk about how we can better become media literate using examples from the real world, not from the classroom.

Learn through example, not theory.

One of the very best ways to learn media literacy is to learn it by example, not through theory. This means accessing many examples of media, and taking the time to examine and question what we are experiencing. The more we stop and think about the media around us, the better we will understand it.

When I teach students about media literacy in my practical media literacy courses, I teach using something called the inquiry method. This just means that I help students learn about the media by teaching them how to ask questions. The thing about asking questions about media is that there is no one right answer. In fact, many students find this frustrating at first. The truth is that what we experience in the media is layered, with many shades of gray in everything we experience. But if we are at least actively thinking about media, trying to understand it by questioning it, we are better off than if we hadn't done so. Questioning our media experiences makes us into critical thinkers, and this skill can easy translate across all different forms of media and beyond!

When learning media literacy, be sure to use examples from television, radio, the Internet, billboards, soda cans, corporate logos on T-shirts, and promotional messages within a media message (like advertising a musical product in a TV show about a young girl rocker). Although these different types of media are different, there will be specific questions you can ask about each medium (angle and lighting in photography, for example), but there are also general questions that you can ask about any media.

There are some essential and basic questions you can ask about any media. I like to compare them to the questions journalists ask when They are researching a story: who, what, where, when, how, why? By asking these questions about media, we can come to many conclusions.

Who – *Who created this message?* This question looks at authorship. Remember that every media message is created, so it has to be created by someone.

Knowing who created the piece of media tells us a lot about that person's or group's values and ideologies. You can also have endless variations on this question. For example, you might ask "what ethnicity or gender is the author of this book, and how does that affect the views represented in it?" You are always asking "who?" by examining the people or groups that created a particular message.

As an example, consider the information we get from websites. How do we know the information is reputable? Just because a website says that something is a fact does not mean it is true. We need to be careful where information comes from – we crave credible information. How do we know if a particular fact is real or was fabricated? When I do research on the internet, I usually try to confirm information I find with a second and third source. I also look for information from reputable websites and original sources.

Extra care should be taken when researching information online. I rarely type in a search term or two and accept the first few results I receive. Just because Google or Bing say that the first few search results are the "top hits," this does not mean those results are necessarily reputable or accurate. Depending on how those search engines rank the list of search results, you can be getting bias search results based on popularity, based on your location or language preference, or based on past search that you or other people made. Combine this with the fact that search engines regularly filter their results, including only results they think you will want, and it is clear that the person doing the searching needs to pay attention to the information They are receiving. It is always worth the time to check more than one or two sources when conducting an online search, and it is also worth searching using more than one search engine. Just because we have access to billions of pieces of information and systems in place to help us search and organize that information, it does not let us off the hook of verifying the information we receive. In fact, I would argue that critical thinking and analysis skills are more in need now than ever before. The simple lesson here: always be willing to dig deeper to find reputable information from reliable sources.

What – *What creative techniques did the message creator use to get my attention?* With this question we are looking at *methods*. Just look at any piece of media and you will notice that each type has its own unique way of communicating an idea. Movies use performance, music, and camera angles to tell a story. Advertisements use persuasion to convince us we want to buy a particular product.

Consider a TV ad for a new action figure. The commercial might show the action figure in action, doing something cool, with a slick high-energy announcer talking about how great the toy is, and with exciting music in the background. All of these elements are what make up a successful toy commercial. As an analogy, the music and announcer are like words, and the whole commercial is like a sentence. The individual elements make up the message as a whole.

Now consider a school textbook that has pictures and big letters. Is this classroom text different than a novel you might read at home? Sure it is. The classroom text uses interesting pictures and big letters to get its audience's attention. As we get older, we tend to like picture books less and in-depth stories more. So as a student's age increases, the number of pictures and the size of the text decrease.

Not to mention that the books get longer as well! This has to do with how the publisher wants to get the intended reader's attention.

Where – Where *was this message placed for my consumption?* Here we are thinking about message placement and target audiences. For example, there is a reason that kids are exposed to fast food restaurant commercials and fun toy commercials during Saturday morning cartoons – it is because kids are likely to respond to these ads. It is the same reason we do not see those same commercials during the evening newscast.

With this question, we are considering the *audience.* Who is the audience and how is the media creator targeting that audience? A textbook has several audiences – the teacher or school that selects the book for classroom use, and of course the student who will use the book. Textbook creators know this so they try to include features that teachers like, but not necessarily features that are conducive to real world learning. Also, teachers select textbooks based on their own worldviews, and based on the worldview they try to provide students. This might mean that certain viewpoints are left out of the text. So with this question we are also questioning *appeal.*

How – *How do I view this message and how might others view it?* In this particular situation we are examining bias and its effect on others. When looking at a media message, it is important to realize that we are looking at it from our own point of view. Each person is different – with different backgrounds, different experiences, different likes and dislikes – and these differences will affect how we view a particular media message. What makes something happy might make someone else sad. What makes one person laugh will make another person cry.

Consider the effect kids have on each other when they say something mean. The kid who said the mean comment may find it funny or may not even think twice about it, while the kid on the receiving end will find it mean and it may make them cry. We see this every day on playgrounds and in classrooms around the world, and usually the kid who said the mean thing is not bothered by upsetting someone else. Now, consider the power the media has to make some people cry or laugh without thinking twice about how others will feel about it. If you are not a part of the offended group, you will not know how it feels to be made fun of. The media has the power to pull on our emotions, and many who create the media messages do not really realize how those messages impact us – or necessarily care.

Why – *Why was this message sent?* In this case, you are questioning intentions. Why did the person or group send you this message? In other words, why did the cartoon producers think it would appeal to kids, and why did they create the characters they did in the way they did? Every piece of media is created for one of two reasons – to sell a product or service (like in an advertisement), or to sell a lifestyle or ideology (music sells the lifestyle the artist lives). Some variations you can have on this question might include "what does the author or creator have to gain by creating this particular piece of media?" Again, as long as you are examining intentions, you are asking the all-important "why?"

Many times, media messages are sent to convince someone of something. Politicians tell us why we should vote for them and not an opponent. Shoe companies tell us why their shoe is worth $100 more than the competitor's. Musicians like to tell us what is cool and what is not, influencing how we dress, how we act, and what types of activities we take part in. TV stations give us shows that we will want to watch so that we can be exposed to the advertisements that help pay their bills.

Every piece of media has an intention behind it. Even this book has an intended purpose – to help you learn practical ways to use and teach media literacy, but also to help me earn an income and gain recognition from my work. But before you dismiss this as a purely financial and egotistical pursuit, consider that there are easier ways to make money and gain recognition than to write a book – so there are other intentions behind this effort to consider, like contributing positively to society. This is also true for teachers – the love of teaching and the act of contributing positively to society are overriding intentions to money and "glory", since these are relatively low in the teaching profession.

Learn using the media that appeals to you.

At schools around the world, students first discuss media and media literacy using the teacher's favorite type of media. This might include using examples from the teacher's favorite newspaper, movie, or advertisement. I disagree with this method, and prefer that people learn about media literacy from media examples that matter to them. This is why in my classes I always begin the year by asking students about their favorite media. I learn all about their favorite movies, musicians, and websites, and then tailor my examples to those preferences. After all, what is the point of learning about media literacy using newspapers or old movies if you will never read a newspaper or watch old movies at home?

Learn media literacy using your preferred media. If you like playing video games, then use the techniques I discuss here and apply them to video games. Do the same thing if you watch lots of YouTube videos, read a lot of Buzzfeed articles, or listen to a lot of music from the 1990s. This way, you will learn the skills of media literacy as they apply to your preferred media, and you will later be able to transfer those skills for use on other types of media, even to newspapers and old movies (if you so choose).

A word about censorship.

A lot has been discussed and debated about the media's influence on young children. A large amount of that debate has dealt with kids and their access to objectionable content – violent video games, risqué movies and TV shows, a vast amount of content online. Many parents and teachers believe that media containing objectionable content should be banned or filtered in schools and in homes kids.

Whenever a fearful parent asks me about what to do about this type of media and how they can protect their kids, I always answer using some sort of analogy. My favorite analogy is the smoking analogy.

Most parents teach their kids that smoking is bad, and that they should not do it. Parents tell the kids about the dangers of smoking, and that if they are caught smoking they will be punished. But what happens when the child goes out into the world and is exposed to people who smoke and who offer them cigarettes? Most kids reject the cigarettes because they have been taught by grownups that cigarettes are bad. Parents with close relationships with their kids can trust them to make the right choice after they have been educated.

Then there are the parents who never tell kids that smoking is bad, or the parents themselves smoke and the kids are exposed to this each day. When the kids go out into the real world they are more likely to do what their parents do, especially if they were never explicitly told that cigarettes are bad. Then if parents find out that their child was smoking, the child is grounded. But what happens the next time the child is out on his or her own?

The same idea applies to media. If parents and teachers assert their values in how they teach kids about media, and they let kids know that there are media out there that they should think twice about viewing, kids will likely listen. At minimum, kids will be aware that there are media out there that they should watch out for. When kids are at a friend's house, where parents have no control over what their kid experiences, kids will likely remember what they learned at home and at school.

These examples show that censorship can only go so far. If parents are upset about a particular TV program, complaining to the station about it will not do anything to help the kid understand what is going on when they experience that TV program at a friend's house or when They are older and have their own TV. Teaching kids to understand the media will help make them more self-reliant, and they will be better able to be critical of media when they do not have parental supervision.

This is why I prefer media literacy to censorship. We teach kids how to interpret their world so when they are out there alone they will know what to do without anyone's help.

Incorporate media literacy in everything you do.

Media are all around us. It does not just sit on the mantle at home or on the desk in the living room. Media are all encompassing – experiences we have thousands of times each day whether we realize it or not. So when we learn media literacy, we should not learn it as an idea that is separate from the rest of our lives, but instead as something that is integral to everything we do.

This book contains lots of examples on how to do this, but the easiest thing you can do to learn media literacy is to just question. Question every piece of media you encounter. The world is the way it is because people allow it to be. If you ask questions about your world, you will soon realize that the world becomes the way you want it to be.

Ask why you see so many commercials when you watch your favorite show. Who put those commercials on your show? Do those commercials benefit you, or do they benefit someone else? What is the alternative to seeing those commercials? How would the world change without commercials?

Ask why everywhere you turn you see another corporate logo. They are everywhere – on TV, on T-shirts, posted at your local stadiums, on billboards, on shoes, on hats, in the classroom, at restaurants. Can we live in a world without corporate logos? Why or why not?

Ask why that news story on TV is at the very beginning of the newscast? Go even further and consider "what is news?" Is news something we need to survive? Is it there to inform us about the world? Is it there to entertain us? Who picks the news stories and the points of view being presented? Do you ever watch the news and think, "I wonder if they will mention this event or that war"? Why do you find the news interesting while others do not?

These are all questions you can ask about the media. Just like I came up with these questions in a short while, I can come up with thousands more about any piece of media – newspapers, TV, radio, websites, blogs, Twitter, songs, clothing, even a telephone call (why do we say "yeah" and "uh huh" when someone is speaking to us on the phone, but we never do that when someone talks to us in person?).

As long as you ask questions, you will come closer to understanding your world. And when you learn how to question, you will be much better prepared to not only handle your media experiences, but also your world in general. Becoming media literate is a gateway to deeper critical thinking abilities.

When you learn to analyze media, you become much better at critical analysis in general. Once you begin learning media literacy, do not be surprised to find that you are better at processing other types of information in your life. You will also become better at recognizing patterns and systems. My own critical analysis abilities have helped me learn several new languages. With each new language, I quickly started to notice patterns and was able to pick up each language much more quickly than other students in my class.

Part 2 – Types of Media

Each type of media has its own unique characteristics and details that make it different from other media. For example, while photography uses lighting, focal length, and framing to tell you its message, radio uses music, sound effects, and voices to give you its messages. In this section we introduce various media and explain what makes each one unique or similar to other types of media. You are encouraged to skip around and focus on the type of media that most interests you. Of course, the more you understand each type of media, the more you will understand media more generally, so you are also encouraged to explore media of all types.

A Note about the Activities in the Following Sections

In the previous section of the book we began to explore the basics of media literacy. We have seen that media literacy is not really this big abstract idea meant to only be understood by graduate students and university professors. Really, it is a process in which we learn to become critical thinkers about both media and society.

Although we have already explored ways to become media literate, we have yet to use concrete examples of how to practice media literacy. Asking questions and being critical about media is a good start, but each type of media contains its own elements that make it special, so it is useful to learn by practicing using these concrete examples.

This section is meant to do just that.

This section has a wide array of activities to teach media literacy covering a variety of different media. Many topics are covered, including news, advertising, television, photography, and more. Each activity covers a specific area of media literacy and gives you a complete workshop-style lesson for each activity, with lesson lengths ranging from 20 minutes to an hour. Everything you need to know in order to analyze media is included – just supply your own media.

As a reminder, there is no right or wrong way to "do media literacy." As such, these activities are just guides to help you along the way. Feel free to change things up and create new activities based on the ones presented here. Also keep in mind that there are no wrong answers in media literacy. Different people will come up with different responses and their own interpretations of the activities presented.

All of the activities can be adapted to account for time constraints. They are also meant to be fun while eye opening at the same time, so start exploring and see what you discover.

Chapter 4 – The Internet – The Web & Social Media

The Internet has provided us with a wealth of information about the world, all at our fingertips. Never in the history of the world has so much information been available so easily to so many people. This has helped make us all smarter, but it has also created a huge problem with information overload.

Today we can search Google and find an answer to any question. The thing is, is it *the right answer*? The reason so much information is available on the Internet is that anybody can create a website with that information. Anybody can add information to Wikipedia. Does that mean that all of this information is correct? Maybe or maybe not. Although sites like Wikipedia have worked to put safeguards in place to protect against blatantly wrong information, this still does not eliminate the possibility of bias. And while much of the information in Wikipedia has become more trustworthy over the years, media literacy in the Internet age is still more important than ever.

We can look to various types of information we receive online. We can look at information from large organizations, for example traditional media outlets that now publish online as well. We can look at new media like blogs and other internet-only media outlets run by just a few people. And then we can also look at social media like the information we receive from websites like Twitter and Facebook. Just because we receive information from our friends or organizations that we follow, that does not mean that the information is correct. In fact, social media has helped spread more misinformation than any other type of media in the history of mankind.

From a media literacy perspective, since the Internet is everywhere and it has so much power to bring us so much information, it is worth paying attention to. Think about how much time you spend online, whether on a website or using a service like Netflix, and even just checking the weather, and you will realize just how deeply connected we are to the internet and its messages.

Social Media – The Interactive Web

Social media are relatively new players in the media landscape, but they have quickly become perhaps the most important players, as it relates to their quick adoption and influence on society. Once called "the interactive web" or "web 2.0", social media are no longer unusual or new, but instead they are part of the very fabric of many people's lives. Who does not log on to Facebook, Twitter, Instagram, or Pinterest at least once a day to see what is new?

Social media started gaining in popularity in the early 2000s with blogs, podcasts, and websites like Myspace, LiveJournal, and Friendster. The main difference between so called "web 1.0" or "the display web" and "web 2.0" sites was that while the older sites just showed information, very similar to how a magazine provides static one way communication, the new sites allowed people to interact with the site and with other people. Whereas the first websites took an approach more like traditional media in which they hired writers, photographers, editors, etc., the new sites simply provided a platform for users to add their own articles, photos, videos, and anything else they could create with their computers. The value of a social media website is the size of its network or user base – the more people that use a particular website, the more popular it becomes.

Today, social media are the main form of personal communication on the internet. And just like more traditional media, we need to be aware that social media companies are there to make money – They are businesses just like movie studios or newspapers. They earn most of the money through advertising, since they would have a lot fewer users if they charged any money at all – remember, their value is the size of their networks. But unlike advertising in traditional, one-direction media, social media websites show you advertising based on information you give them. They know about you because you give them your age, your location, and you tell them what you like. So they know a lot about you, and this has concerned many privacy groups. However, we are at a point that most people in our society feel that many of these websites – Facebook and Google likely being the most prominent – are vital to our everyday lives, so we accept some loss in privacy for the privilege to use the site and to connect with our friends.

Social media has been a double-edged sword, both for the spread of ideas and information in society, as well as for democracy itself. Its power can be seen in the fact that Donald Trump uses Twitter nearly every day to communicate directly with his constituents, as well as with the traditional media. However, many issues arise with social media, not in the least being the fact that social media exacerbates the other issues mentioned here, such as creating an echo chamber, taking advantage of click bait, and allowing for a certain amount of anonymity among its users.

Twitter, once considered a minor social network compared to industry leader Facebook, resurged in popularity with the election of Donald Trump as president. Twitter is now seen as the preferred social network for discussing news and politics, with groups of users often battling each other in the comments of popular tweets. Twitter's users can be subdivided into three main groups: newsmakers such as the President and other politicians, journalists and commentators of news and current events, and anonymous users who take part in the "Twitter Wars" in the comments of political tweets.

Twitter's resurgence has fueled the accelerated rise of divisiveness in America by putting its users in two main factions: for Trump and against Trump. The anonymous nature of Twitter allows regular people to battle others with words they would never use in real life. The anonymity helps bring out people's worst impulses.

On the other hand, Twitter initially helped spread the #BlackLivesMatter and #MeToo movements, so its use as a platform for change should not be completely discarded. Twitter was also instrumental in other political and social movements, including Occupy Wall Street and the Arab Spring, which saw Twitter being used as a way for organizers to communicate without government interference.

In addition to its use as a platform for communication of political dissidents and also for spreading new political ideologies, Twitter is home for many otherwise-under-represented communities. One such community is the *Black Twitter* community, a corner of Twitter which enables communication among those in the African American community. Black Twitter participants contribute to discussions on everything from who is running for president to memes about Beyoncé.

While Twitter has managed to become a platform for discussion with limited user accountability, but capable of starting and sustaining political movements, anonymity is one of the key factors that drives discussion on another popular social media site, Reddit.

Internet Anonymity

The back in the early days of the World Wide Web, the internet supported the idea that participation could be, at least to some degree, anonymous. While major internet companies have shifted away from anonymity, with many requiring a real name and/or phone number as a way of verifying users, the social media site Reddit, along with a several others have gone in the opposite direction, allowing its members to post and comment anonymously, without as much as needing to use a verified e-mail address. This has lead to the site being seen as a breeding ground for hate speech and which supports the espousing of extremist views.

Reddit has forums called sub-Reddits, or "subs", with each focused on a particular topic, such as "politics" and even "cats". While most of these subs are innocuous, many seem to bring out the racists and bigots of the internet. Each sub has a moderator, or many if it has many readers, but policing is mostly handled through a points system called "Karma". For each person who agrees with your post or comment, an upvote gives you positive Karma, while a downvote will give you negative Karma. Comments with negative Karma are usually collapsed and relegated to the bottom of the comments feed. While the system sounds like a positive method of self-governance, Karma leads to group think mentality, with people piling on Karma one way or the other.

While the Karma system on Reddit seems benign, it is only when one finds themselves commenting on sensitive topics, that its true nature is unleashed. For example, the sub called "The_Donald" had (it has since been banned by Reddit) numerous racist and sexist posts from Donald Trump supporters, and these posts frequently receive thousands of upvotes, qualifying them to be considered for Reddit's front page, where it is likely to receive more attention and followers.

Audience Fragmentation

When your audiences are so divided that one audience's truth looks nothing like a different audience's truth, you have audience fragmentation. This was the case at the start of 2016 (and even earlier) when we read about Donald Trump supporters getting different messages from social media than people who were considered liberal or progressive. The algorithms that social media companies use to keep us coming back and "doom-scrolling," for messages that appeal to them. In my own experiments, starting a new Twitter account and following Donald Trump lead Twitter to instantly recommend people I should follow. These were other conservatives and allies of President Trump. The more I added these suggested people, the more I was able to discover so called "alt-right" Twitter, a messy corner of Twitter where vaccines are evil, and Hillary Clinton is part of a deep-state conspiracy. Starting another new Twitter account and starting by following the Democratic National Committee, I was offered suggestions to follow the New York Times,

Bernie Sanders, Joe Biden, and many more left-leaning personalities and news outlets.

Hopefully you can clearly see the problem here. If I am of one side or another (or even someone who considers themselves "green" or "libertarian"), over time, I will read my Twitter feed and it will present a perspective of the world that is unique to me and "my people." This has disastrous effects in attempts at unity and people sharing a common cause. This is much different than in the 1970s and even into the 1980s, when people only had three networks from which to get their news, at most maybe a few local newspapers, and perhaps one radio station for local news and talk. Back then, the country was not so divided, and this was mostly a good thing. Today our information is so segmented that it segments us. In fact, if I set up my Twitter just right, I can spend all day scrolling and never encounter an idea that I disagree with or that challenges my view on reality.

Let us talk about some key elements of social media sites to try to understand them better. These are some characteristics that belong to all social media sites, although they are implemented in different ways from site to site.

Elements of the interactive web

1. User-Generated Content

Social media are set apart from other media, and especially other internet media, by the fact that social media websites and apps are considered *platforms*, meaning that users provide the content for the service, not the company itself. This aspect is so important to the idea of social media, that user-generated content is really the most definitive element of this type of media.

User-generated content can be seen on every social media website – your status update on Facebook, the photo you pin on Pinterest, the item you buy or sell on eBay, and the chat you initiate on Whatsapp. In each scenario, the social media company is providing a platform for you to participate in a variety of activities, yet they are not creating any content themselves – Facebook itself does not post other people's status updates (of course Facebook as a company has its own Facebook page!), Pinterest itself does not pin any photos to their walls, eBay does not sell any items that they have produced or purchased, and Whatsapp does not chat with you directly. The company provides software for you to do this, and for you to interact with other people.

2. User Interaction

As just mentioned, interaction among users is an important part of social media's inner workings. Facebook, for example, would be useless if none of your friends used it. So the value of Facebook is not in how cool or easy the software is, but how big their network is. Similarly, eBay is not about the number of features it has, but how many people are willing to buy and sell merchandise on the website. This element of social media is key to understanding how these services work, and how they interact with users. As an example, Facebook is just about the only place online where we can connect with all of our friends – it seems everyone we know is on Facebook. And because Facebook's network of users is so large, it has the power to do things we may not agree with. In recent years, many users have become concerned with how Facebook uses our information and how it protects (or does not protect) our privacy. Since Facebook has a large network – allowing people to connect with all of their friends – it has some power to make chances to its policies while expecting little push back from users. In a way, we are forced to accept giving up certain freedoms in order to continue connecting with our friends. This is key to understanding the power of social media and online social networks.

3. Democratization of Information

Another important element of social media we need to understand is how it helps make information democratic – anyone, anywhere, at any time can write or record something and upload it to a website or app for the world to see. In the days when magazines and newspapers ruled, readers could write letters to the editors and have their opinions published, but even then someone was deciding which letters were published and which were not. Today, even online news and information outlets allow its users to post comments that are published immediately without any editorial review. This is great in many ways, the most important of which is that minority points of views do not get overlooked and we end up with more voices in every conversation. A huge downside to this is that we sometimes read and see things we do not see as acceptable. While most people are well intentioned with their posts or comments, a small number of people use these new outlets to spew hatred or engage in cyber bullying. In recent years we have seen an increase in the years of Twitter as an outlet popular with cyber bullies to attack people they disagree with. We have also seen a rise of terrorist groups like ISIS using Twitter to recruit people and to spread their message of violence. The freedoms we have gained with social media has turned out to be a double-edged sword that we need to explore in depth to understand it fully.

4. Collective Intelligence

The fact that many people are interacting on social media means that there is now a market of ideas online – with so many people freely discussing ideas and issues, the collective internet can often come to a consensus on how to think. Take Yelp as an example. Yelp helps people find good restaurants by letting users rate their dining experiences, and allowing others to view those ratings and read the accompanying reviews. The more people that rate a particular restaurant, the more likely that rating is to be accurate. As an example, let us say you are looking for an Italian restaurant at which to have dinner. You use search Yelp and find two nearby

Italian restaurants, one with five stars and three reviews, and one with four stars and 230 reviews. Which one of the ratings for these two restaurants do you think would be more likely to be accurate? If you said the one with four stars and 230 reviews, then you would be correct. The reason is that more people have visited and reviewed that restaurant, so the occasional rating from a really happy or a really angry user is likely to be balanced with all of the more fair ratings. This is just one example of collective intelligence, and we see it everywhere in social media, including edits that lead to accurate articles on Wikipedia, interactions leading to popular tweets and hashtags on Twitter, and up votes leading to good answers to questions on Quora.

5. No Price Of Admission

The final defining aspect of social media is that these services never charge users to use the basic features of the website or app. When just starting up, social media companies take money from investors in order to grow their number of users quickly, and they then sell advertising to companies who want to show their ads to the service's users. The reason they never charge users to use their services is because fewer people would use social media websites and apps if users had to pay for them. As a parallel, consider how many people watch broadcast television compared to how many people subscribe to HBO or Netflix. Broadcast television is available for free and is supported by advertisements while HBO and Netflix charge monthly fees, so those paid services only have a fraction of the users of broadcast TV. The same is true with Social Media. Imagine if Facebook charged its users to access the website. Maybe a few of your friends would be there, but not all of them. Remember earlier I mentioned that the value of these social media services is in the size of their networks, so Facebook would be worthless if all of your friends were not using it.

For an example of why this is so important, we can look at an early social media website called Classmates.com. This website allowed people to connect to past classmates by having them fill in their school information. When I first discovered the website, I was able to find several of my grade school classmates, but I had to pay for a subscription if I wanted to contact any of them. I was frustrated about this, and after thinking it over for a few minutes, I decided not to pay. Luckily, Facebook came along a few years later, and I quickly reconnected with several classmates free of charge. Facebook is now the largest social network in the world and one of the most popular websites on the internet, while Classmates.com... is not.

Of course, since we are not paying for the services that connect us to our friends, the cost is that we give up some privacy and information to Facebook's advertisers so that they can target their ads at specific users. Sometimes I find it creepy when an ad appears in Facebook feed that seems like it was created just for me (Facebook knows my city, my birthday, the things I like, and the games I play), but I am willing to allow this in order to connect to my friends. However, if Facebook had a reliable competitor that also had many of my friends on it, Facebook would likely be more responsive to user privacy concerns and the ads would likely be less creepy.

The following are a variety activities that will help you start to understand how online media works, and how it is different from other types of media.

ACTIVITY: Website Authorship (Personal Site)

What you need: A website created by an individual, not a company. You can find a website like this by going to blogger.com or wordpress.com.

How long it takes: It takes about five minutes to find a website or two, about five minutes to read the website, and about 10-15 minutes to analyze the website.

What it teaches: This activity teaches that each person has their own perspective and point of view, and that this perspective comes out whenever they write online.

The activity: Take a look at an informational website that was NOT created by a company. Why did the author create the site? Who is the website's audience? Is the author trying to sell you something? Is the site's content affected by what the author has for sale on the website? Is the author trying to convince you of their point of view? Is the information on the website factual? How do you know? Try searching another website by a different author and check to see if the information is the same or different.

What is going on: Each person has their own point of view, their own beliefs, and their own ways of thinking about the world. Someone who writes their own website usually has something they want to say to the world. Usually they are trying to present their point of view on a particular topic. Websites that are run by individuals rather than companies have no editorial process or filtering process to be sure that information is correct or that information is unbiased. The writer of the website is usually trying to convince you of their point of view so that you will take some action; usually they want you to believe what they believe, but often times they want you to buy something. If the author makes some claims about some particular topic and these claims seem incorrect or different from when you had previously known, it may be worth it to check another source to verify that information.

ACTIVITY: Website Authorship (Commercial Site)

What you need: An informational website created by a company or other organization.

How long it takes: It takes about five minutes to find a website or two, about five minutes to read the website, and about 10-15 minutes to analyze the website

What it teaches: The purpose of a company is to sell you a product or service. Companies with websites use those websites to reach out to customers and convince them to buy that product or service.

The activity: Take a look at an informational website created by a company. Why did the company create the site? Is the site's main purpose to give you information or to sell you a product or service? Does the site contain advertising? Could the advertiser influence the information on the site? For example, is the author careful not to say something bad about an advertised product? Does the information relate to a product the company is trying to sell you?

What is going on: Companies cannot exist without sales. Companies trying to sell people their products and services through their websites use marketing text to convince you to buy. The marketing text that the website uses was carefully written and rewritten by professionals with the purpose of convincing you to buy the product or service. Often times the information on a commercial website excludes information that could weaken the sales pitch, while emphasizing information that will strengthen the sales pitch. You should be aware that information on a commercial website is not unbiased but instead is there to make you part with your money in exchange for their product or service. Become aware of the tactics used by these companies so that you can then better prepare yourself and really decide if you need that product or service, or if the company is just doing a really good job of convincing you that you do. These websites will often present you with information about the product or service, and provide you with a way to purchase it either through a link or with an ad.

ACTIVITY: Information Search

What you need: A computer with an Internet connection and web browser. Point the web browser to a popular search engine – Google and Bing are the search engines most used by students.

How long it takes: This exercise takes approximately 30 minutes to complete.

What it teaches: How to find reliable information about a topic that you are researching, and how to filter out search results that are not credible.

The activity: Use a search engine to research a topic that interests you. Find two or three different websites that talk about that topic. Before accepting the information presented to you, ask yourself some questions about that information. What is the website you are receiving this information from? Who was responsible for writing the information on the site (an individual? A company? A non-profit?)? How is the author connected to the information on the website? Is the author an expert on the topic you are researching? How would you know if the author is an expert or not? Who does the author work for, and how does that influence the information on the site? If the author works for an organization, how is that organization connected to the information? Does the website sell anything, and if so, is the information on the site somehow connected to the hope that you will buy something from them? Is the information on the website accurate? How would you know if the information is accurate? Do any parts of the information seem inaccurate? Look at the other websites and ask yourself these same questions. How do the websites compare? Does one appear to be better than another? Why?

What is going on: Search engines give you results on a topic you are searching for, but the search engine has no way of knowing that the information on the resulting website is accurate, complete, or unbiased. In fact, the only reason you are seeing a particular search result at the top after your search is because that search result is popular in some way – perhaps that website is visited a lot, or maybe a lot of people link to that particular page. The result is that your search query may return search results that are popular with other web searchers, but is not necessarily accurate. As a prudent researcher, you should always check your information using several sources. After having read the first couple of search results, check the next few results to verify the information. If the information does not match, ask yourself why this is the case. Maybe some information is outdated, or maybe some information is biased in some way.

ACTIVITY: Wikipedia

What you need: A computer with an Internet connection and web browser. Point the web browser to Wikipedia.

How long it takes: This exercise takes approximately 30 minutes to complete.

What it teaches: How to find and recognize accurate information on Wikipedia, how to avoid potentially incorrect information, and how to detect bias in the information in an article.

The activity: Use Wikipedia to research a topic that interests you and that you are already somewhat familiar with. Read through the article and note the facts that the text claims about the subject. Does this information seem correct? How do you know if the information is correct? Are the facts accompanied by references at the bottom? Do those references seem credible? Are the facts verifiable through a secondary source (for example, does a second source found through a search engine agree with the fact in question?)? Are there any facts in the article that are in dispute (not wrong, but perhaps not verified or generally unknown)?

What is going on: Wikipedia is the most used internet source of information and is used by millions of students each day for research projects. In the past, Wikipedia was viewed by many in the academic community as an unreliable source of information, since anyone was allowed to edit the information in an article. This made it possible to find wrong information, and even malicious or slanderous information in Wikipedia articles. The site's developers have gone to great lengths to make the information more reliable (adding article curators, adding a revision history, requiring an account to edit information, and requiring citations for any facts). Still, the information on Wikipedia should be verified using additional sources when possible. Although many of the problems that lead to inaccuracies have been improved upon, the information on Wikipedia is still curated by humans – and all humans have a bias whether we realize it or not. In short, it is always best to use additional sources to verify any piece of information, whether the information was originally found on Wikipedia, or anywhere else.

ACTIVITY: Social Media Advertising

What you need: A computer with an Internet connection and web browser. Point the web browser to a either Facebook or Twitter and login.

How long it takes: This exercise takes approximately 30 minutes to complete.

What it teaches: This exercise makes us aware of just how much information sites like Facebook and Twitter have about us. With so much concern over user privacy and the use of our information, we should know just how these social media companies use our information.

The activity: Navigate to your homepage on either Facebook or Twitter. Now, examine the advertising shown to you on just your homepage and news feed. Make a list of the various advertisements and then ask yourself some questions about them. Why did the site show you these ads? Are you interested in the products or services being advertised? Why or why not? How do the advertisements try to convince you to click on them? Do they entice you with something free? Do they say that one (or several) of your friends already like that product or service? If the website knows about you before showing you these ads, what do you think it says about you that you were shown this ad instead of an ad for something else? Would you click on any of these ads? Why or why not?

What is going on: Social media sites like Facebook and Twitter have very sophisticated ways of knowing about you by the friends you are connected to, the pages you like, the posts you have made, and the comments you have left for other people. This information is not a secret to the website, and they use this information to allow advertisers to target specific messages to you that they think you will want to click on. Many people get upset when they learn that this is going on, but you have to consider that Facebook and Twitter are not really free. Sure, you do not pay anything to them, but they need to make money somehow so they sell advertisements to companies that want to sell something to someone like you. Those companies never get your actual information (unless you like a page, then they will know your name), but they see you as a specific piece of a target market, and they want to sell you something. For example, advertisers on Facebook can show an advertisement just to people who are male, age 18 to 20, who live in California, and who like punk music. That is a very specific group of people, and it can only be done because Facebook knows all of this about you based on what you post, what you like, and what you fill out in your profile.

Chapter 5 – Visual Media – TV, Movies, & Streaming

It is incredible to think about television and movies as so-called traditional media. Although these forms of media have been around for a very long time, the content we receive from them today seems fresh and interesting while simultaneously feeling established and a bit old fashioned. Streaming services have not only breathed new life into motion media, but they are helping to redefine just what we call a television show or a movie. In a world where you can watch the latest Hollywood hits alongside funny cat videos on screens ranging from four inches to 100 inches, we realize just how far we have come with media technology.

So what do movies and television shows of yesterday have in common with the video we stream today? We can start at a basic level by describing what they all have in common (besides the fact that they are all shown on screens) – they are all considered entertainment.

What is Entertainment?

When we think about why we use media in general – why we read a book or magazine, listen to the radio, or browse the internet – the reasons for doing so range from wanting to get informed or connect with friends, or just having something to do to pass the time. In short, we want to be entertained. Media producers know this fact, so they incorporate entertainment in everything they make.

Here is an example of how entertainment is intertwined with so many of our media experiences. Think about how we prefer to get our news. Let us say that there was a robbery at a local bank. The news story is simple – the robbers came in, demanded the money, and then left and have not been found. If I was an eye witness and told you the whole story, it would take me about 30 seconds in total. This story is out there for anyone to tell – newspapers will publish the story, and local TV stations will talk about it during their news programs. Now imagine you are in the news division at a local TV station. You want people to watch your station for news on the robbery. But why would anyone watch your TV station if they can get the same information anywhere else? The answer is that people will watch your news program for more reasons than just the story. They will watch your station because you provide the best entertainment. This may be because you have the most attractive news anchors, or because you have the nicest graphics or the most engaging music. Essentially, TV stations add a lot of interesting elements to their news programs so that you will choose them over another station.

In the entertainment industry, there is a large focus on owning "properties" – unique content that no one else can use and that will help you get viewers. Take Disney as an example. They own many properties, but probably their most famous is Mickey Mouse. They get to decide how and when you get to see Mickey, and that helps them have an edge over their competition (other animation studios). TV shows are properties, as are movies and comic books. The TV news show is a property as well – adding in the attractive anchors, slick graphics and music all add to the uniqueness that will help get them viewers.

Television

Many of us do not know of a time in our lives without television. Since we were young, we have sat in front of it, allowing it to teach us about the world. Before television, the world was full of mystery, with media bringing to us only its most interesting and appealing content. But television changed the way we consume media. It also changed the way we experience life.

Television has brought us many great things. After all, where else could we experience live moving images from around the world, as well as from just around the corner? Television introduced us to outer space, far away lands, and the Beatles. It shows us far away places, makes us laugh and cry, and keeps us informed about current events. Television is a time machine, a teacher, and yes, even a baby sitter.

But for all of its wonders, television has also received extensive criticism for its shortcomings. Television is often cited as being the "boob tube" that makes us less intelligent, minimizing details and relying heavily on stereotypes to tell us its stories. Television is seen as the preferred method for advertisers and storytellers to tell us about the "bad things" in life.

Sex, drugs, violence, and alcohol are everywhere on television, and some believe these televised depictions will only get worse.

Is television the best media ever invented, or the worst? Does it do more good or bad for society? Although it would be difficult to answer those questions, it is safe to say that television is certainly the most influential type of media. This was true in the 20th century, and it is also true thus far in the 21st century. So instead of putting down its shortcomings, or praising its accomplishments, why not take a different perspective?

Consider looking at television as simply a medium. A medium worth analyzing and worth making careful observations about. Let us think about television – how it works, how it affects us, how it has changed out world, and how television itself is changing. This way, we can decide, not if television is good or bad, but ultimately, how it affects our individual lives positively or negatively. The answer is a complex one.

Television as Entertainment

One way of thinking about television and its influence on us is to think of it as a way to entertain us. You will soon discover that everything on television – from news to sports, and from Saturday morning educational shows to the latest season of House of Cards – are all there for our entertainment. So let us frame our discussion thinking about entertainment as the main idea behind what we see on TV.

Movies as Entertainment

One way of thinking about movies and their influence on us is to think of them as ways to entertain us. Although some movies may have deep messages about our society and some may even make us think about our own lives, ultimately a movie must be entertaining in order to appeal to us. No one will go see a movie that has an earth-shattering message if it also is not entertaining. This is why it is worth framing our discussion of movies around the idea of movies as entertainment. Using this perspective will help us more readily identify the various elements of movies.

TV and Movies – Content Revolves Around Genre

When we think about the types or categories of TV shows and movies that exist, we are really thinking about genres. A genre is a set of conventions or rules that help place entertainment into categories. A TV show's genre tells you a lot about the show itself – what kind of stories are being told, what kind of characters will we encounter, what kind of people will want to watch this show, and much more.

There are too many genres to list here, but I will give you an example of one we see often on TV: the reality show. The basic rules of this genre are that they should show real people as themselves and in realistic situations. Although the situations can be artificially created by the producers, the cameras are there solely to capture these real people participating in these situations. These are the basic rules of a reality show – if one or more of these basic rules are not met, for example if the characters are actors playing other people, then instantly this is no longer a reality show. Of course, we can go beyond the basics and add other elements. For example, a game show is a type of reality show in which real people compete for prizes. Game show producers create an artificial environment, for example an obstacle course like in ABC's Wipeout, and then they let us watch these real people trying to get through the course.

Some other popular genres in entertainment are drama, comedy, romance, horror, action, adventure, and crime drama. Take a moment to think about your favorite TV show and consider what genre it might be a part of. What elements about the show tell you that it is a part of one genre instead of another?

Genres can say a lot about the people who enjoy them. For example, think about the types of people who enjoy horror movies. With their violence, constant scares, and depictions of overt sexuality, it is no wonder that teenagers are the primary audience for films and shows in this genre. Filmmakers know this, so they write their films to appeal to them. This is typically done by filling scripts with stereotypes that appeal to specific audience members. Consider your favorite genre of movies or TV shows, and think about why it appeals to you. What does it say about you as a media consumer? What types of characters, stories, themes, and cultural references are used to appeal to you?

Characters on TV and in Movies

The types of characters we see on TV and in movies are typically based on familiar types or personas that seem familiar to us. Most modern Western movies have a main character, sometimes called the protagonist or hero. Throughout the story, that main character is somehow in conflict with another main character, sometimes called the antagonist or villain. The story often has supporting characters that either help or block the protagonist from reach his or her goal.

The most obvious example of these character types can be seen in super hero movies. Iron Man, our hero, battles his evil nemesis and saves the world. Along the way, Iron Man is helped by Penny, without whom he would not be able to win the day. Although it is easy to recognize the hero and villain in a super hero movie, most movies and TV shows contain characters that follow this formula. In horror movies, the protagonist is the people we follow through the story, and the antagonist is the monster trying to kill those people. In a romantic comedy, these roles are even more subtle – the protagonist is usually either one person in the relationship and the antagonist is the other person in the relationship. Whoever we meet first and follow most is usually the protagonist.

Characters can be very complex, as we see in adult dramas. These characters are not completely good or bad, but somewhere in the middle. These are what we call well-rounded characters. They have internal conflicts and they struggle with who they are. We typically see flat characters – the pure good or pure evil – in super hero films.

Stories on TV and in Movies

The stories we see on TV and in movies are based on story concepts and structures that go back to ancient storytelling, some of which we even see in the bible. In recent years, these story concepts and structures have been well defined for us by author Chris Voegler, in his book, The Hero's Journey. This book is itself a sort of bible for movie and TV producers, who use Voegler's ideas to create stories that appeal to us on an emotional level.

Let me tell you a story. A woman enjoys her life – she has a good job, a loving family, and everything is going great for her. Suddenly, she loses her job (or her family, or anything else important to her), and she enters a new world where she needs to adjust. She faces obstacles, things get worse, and she is about to give up. Before giving up, something changes – something she set into motion earlier – and she suddenly knows how to get her life back on track. She confronts her main obstacle (her ex-boss, her husband, the nosy mailman), and her life gets back on track, except now she is changed for the better and she is a stronger person. Does this story sound familiar? If it does, that is because it is a structure used by most storytellers today.

Let me tell you another story. A young man is orphaned as a child and lives with his aunt and uncle. Things are going ok, but he wants more out of his life. He feels stuck. Out of nowhere, his family is killed and he is thrown into a whole new world. He faces obstacles, and things get worse along the way. Just when he is about to give up, something happens that sets him on a collision course with the person that caused him all of this pain. He confronts that person, defeats him, and returns home as a hero and a better person. Does this story sound familiar? It should – it is the story to Star Wars.

Try this with exercise with your favorite movie or television series (in TV this usually happens over several seasons from beginning to end). Can you tell when the main character leaves his or her ordinary world for the new world? What event caused this change in the protagonist's life? How does the character struggle, and how does he or she get through it? Can you find the point when they are about to give up, but suddenly they figure out a plan? What happens when they confront the antagonist? Trust me, it is all there in most modern stories on television and in movies.

Elements of TV Shows and Movies

Most of us know how to identify a TV show or movie when we see one, but have you ever stopped to think about what is the actual definition of a TV show or a movie? What must a movie contain in order to be considered a movie? How long is too long for a TV show? When is a TV show really a movie? How can we tell the difference? For example, is a 3-minute video shot on your smartphone and uploaded to YouTube a movie? Why or why not? What about a 90-minute video of a fireplace that you can watch on your television at home – is that a movie? Can a movie be shot on video, or does it need to be shot on film to be a movie? Can a movie make its first appearance on Netflix without first going into theaters? Can a TV show be a series of short episodes on YouTube? These are just some things you can ask yourself to begin thinking of the elements that make up a TV show or a movie. The following are just some of the generally accepted elements of episodic TV shows and movies:

Script

All episodic (non-reality) TV shows and movies are based on some sort of script or structure that helps guide the audience from beginning to end. While this is very easy to identify in a fictional film like Iron Man or 12 Years a Slave – these movies are based off of a script written by a screenwriter – it is not as easy to identify the presence of a script in a documentary like An Inconvenient Truth or The Cove. But even documentaries have story editors that help tell a story from beginning to end using the footage they shot. Some filmmakers in recent years have tried using improvisation and allowing the story to unfold organically using the input from the actors, but even these types of movies have a general guide of where they want to go in their stories. Despite the popularity of so called “unscripted” reality television, episodic television still has very high viewership.

Message

Every television show and movie has a message, whether you realize it or not. The message could be “true love lasts a lifetime” (Titanic), “the financial industry ruined the economy” (Inside Job), or “power makes people do anything to keep it or have more of it” (House of Cards), but every TV show and movie has a core message. Think about your favorite movie – what is the message that it conveys to the audience? If you have watched a television series from the beginning, do you know what the ongoing theme of the show is? Understanding the underlying message is a critical thinking skill tied to media literacy. If you can understand the message, you can then decide whether to accept that message or deny it instead.

Recording

TV shows and movies are recorded on some audio-visual medium such as film or video. The action is captured by one or several cameras, and then edited together before being shown to the audience. While television shows and YouTube videos undergo this process, often movies use more complex recording methods that also include adjusting the lighting, framing shots and camera angles to create something best experienced on a big screen.

Length

A movie can be of any length – short movies can be as short as a few seconds, and anthologies can be 10 hours or longer – but in general, the vast majority of movies released in the past 50 years are between 85 and 125 minutes in length. Length is also dependent on the movie's genre or category. Comedies are more likely to be shorter (around 90-100 minutes), while dramas are likely to be longer (around 110-120 minutes).

A television show is typically either 30 minutes or 60 minutes in length, including commercial interruptions. As more and more television-type shows appear online, this old-fashion rule is quickly disappearing. Netflix original series episodes often last approximately 50 minutes each, while the episodes of a web series on YouTube could be as short as five minutes.

Distribution

Movies are commonly released in movie theaters before ending up on pay-per-view television or on Netflix, but this is quickly changing. Digital distribution has made it easy for movie makers and movie studios to release their movies directly to audiences through online outlets like Amazon Instant Video, iTunes, Google Play, or Netflix. This has made it easier and more cost effective for movie producers to create something interesting and try to reach a more specific audience than mainstream movies. Promotion is a large part of distribution, and the bigger budget movies need to be promoted widely in order to reach a mass audience. This is still best accomplished through movie theaters, but this will change once more people have access to broadband and internet-connected televisions.

Television shows originally only aired on television. Even the term "to air" means that the show is transmitted by antenna from a broadcast tower to a television. Although most television comes over cables now (either from your cable or satellite company, or through your broadband internet connection), we still say that a show *airs* on some channel or website.

Cast and Crew

Television shows and movies are not cheap to make, mainly because they require the work of many people to bring them into existence. The cast are the people who appear on camera – they could be actors, documentary subjects, or even animated characters. The crew are the people behind the scenes. The director figures out what shots to record and how to organize those shots, the producer plans the shoots and maintains a budget, the writer writes the episodes or movie and makes changes at the director's or producer's request, the editor edits the raw footage and assembles it to help tell the director's story, and many more people take care of a vast amount of important details.

Individually, none of the elements mentioned here can be said to be unique to television shows or movies. But taken together, the elements we just described help describe them in general. Of course, we must also take into account how technology makes us think about television and movies.

The following are a variety activities that will help you start to understand how television and movies work, and how they are different from other types of media.

Appendix: Television-related Learning Activities

ACTIVITY: TV Commercials

What you need: A little imagination, some paper and writing instruments, and the name of a few companies with popular products that target the people in your group.

How long it takes: The setup takes about 5 minutes, the design portion takes about 20-30 minutes, and the presentations and discussion take about 5 minutes per commercial.

What it teaches: The commercial messages around us, especially television commercials, do not sell us products but instead market solutions for better lives. Instead of selling us on product features like construction quality and price, many products are sold by telling us how much better they will make us feel, how many more people will like us, and how much better we will be as people if we only buy the product. Some commercials are more subtle, while others are very overt.

The activity: The students in the group will get into small groups of two or three people each. Each group will be presented with a piece of paper containing an image of a popular product targeted towards this group. Then, ask the students to create a concept for a television commercial for this product. Ask them to keep in mind who the target market is, and how the target market will benefit from using this product. Ask them to think beyond the product's physical characteristics, and to consider the ideas behind the product. How can the product be sold emotionally to its market, rather than rationally or practically? Have the students create the concept for the product, and then draw a six-box storyboard for the commercial, with one portion of the story in each consecutive box.

Give the students about 20-30 minutes to come up with their ideas, and then regroup and present each storyboard. Be sure to ask, "who is the target market for this product/commercial," "what problem does the product solve," "what makes this product different from its competition," "could the product appeal to a different target audience but is not being marketed to them," and "are stereotypes used in selling this product to customers?"

What is going on: Nearly all products are sold using commercials that appeal to us on an emotional level. Rarely is a product sold because of its physical attributes. For example, a pencil is usually never sold with an advertisement saying "made of top quality recycled timber with a polyurethane eraser and a sturdy construction", but instead is usually sold as "reliable and dependable to help get you through your tests." Commercials have a short time to connect with their audiences, and so they need to quickly answer the question "what is in it for the buyer?"

This is especially true for products that have many competitors. Companies use branding as a way to tell customers, "this logo means you will receive this guaranteed experience." A prime example of this is with energy drink products. There are many similar products in this category, all with similar effects and similar tasting liquids. So how do these companies make themselves stand out? They market their products using emotion rather than practical usage. As soon as you see the packaging, you will know who the product is being sold to. A large black can is aimed towards men, while a smaller pink can is aimed towards women, while yet another light blue can is aimed towards a more affluent market. There is even an energy drink named after an illicit drug, which aims to capitalize on the adolescent curiosity of drug use. All of these products have the same effect, contain products with a similar flavor, but they are made to appeal to customers based on emotion rather than practical uses.

Since television commercials have so little time to capture our attention, they need to increase the emotional impact of their ads. They use characters, visuals, music, and atmosphere that appeal to their target audience. If a commercial does a good job of selling you the product, then you can likely see yourself in the commercial's main character or in the situation the character finds himself in.

ACTIVITY: Reality Shows

What you need: Your imagination, a piece of paper and a writing instrument.

How long it takes: The setup takes about 5 minutes, the design portion takes about 20-30 minutes, and the presentations and discussion take about 5 minutes per reality show.

What it teaches: Reality shows claim to depict reality, but they really only depict a hyper-reality – a reality constructed by a video editor meant to show the most sensational parts. Reality show producers only include video that appeals to the show's target audience, fits within the given time constraints, and will guarantee viewership.

The activity: Develop a reality show based on your own life. Decide on a target audience and include only those portions of your life that will appeal to your audience. A good way to figure out who is in your target audience is to consider on what cable station your show would air on. Since cable stations tightly target their audiences (for example, "black men, ages 18-21, who enjoy popular music"), you could easily find a station that may somewhat reflect your own target market.

Name your show and consider your content. What aspects of your life would the show include? Why do you think that part of your life is interesting? Who is the target audience for your show? Why would your target audience want to watch your show over another show on television? Because you are only including a certain aspect of your life, does the show truly reflect you as a whole person?

What is going on: Reality show producers often create an unnatural situation for the people on the show to live in. Sometimes these shows involve contests, or otherwise making the participants take part in some activity that is not a part of daily life. Even shows that just follow someone around so that the audience could experience their exciting life are usually making the people do things they would not normally do, just for the camera's sake.

A once-popular reality show about dating would often end with the would-be couple using a hot tub – the producer's decision to appeal to the show's young audience. Another once-popular show about the lives of young real estate agents would rarely depict scenes that did not cover some aspect of their careers. Another show about a rock star's family life had self-contained episodes, making it seem that each week the family tackled another whacky issue that seemed to work itself out by the end of the hour.

All of these situations can be seen as "constructed reality" instead of real reality, the way things really happen in real life. Several people were involved in the task of editing down hundreds of hours of footage into a one-hour episode. Producers, video editors, tape loggers, and story editors all work together to construct the show's world. The result is flat caricatures that rarely resemble the lives or personalities of real people. This helps create a false impression about the lifestyle of the people in the show, and helps perpetuate stereotypes about celebrities and people in general.

Appendix: Movie-related Learning Activities

ACTIVITY: Movie Development

What you need: Something to write out ideas on; a pen and paper or a computer.

How long it takes: This exercise can take anywhere from 45 minutes to an hour and a half to complete, depending on the amount of time given to students to work, and how long students have to present their ideas.

What it teaches: This exercise teaches how to recognize the elements of a successful movie, and helps us realize that movies are a business as well as an art form.

The activity: Develop an idea for a movie that you think will be a huge success in theatres. Write a one or two sentence summary of the story, and then determine what actors will play the main characters. Then develop a tag line or phrase that will help sell the movie to audiences. Finally, put together a poster for the movie using the tagline. Why do you think the movie will be successful? Why did you choose those actors for your movie instead of other actors? What is so interesting about your tagline that will get people interested in the movie? What makes your poster so appealing to the movie's audience? Present your ideas to the group.

What is going on: We find movies interesting because they tell us stories using visuals, action, and drama. In many ways, we have come to expect certain things from the movies we go see. An action movie should have a lot of action and not many long dramatic speeches. The actors in dramas should be well respected and perhaps even award winning. We have expectations, and we expect the movies we watch to meet those expectations. This means that movie producers try to give us what they think we want, and rarely try to challenge our way of thinking. So it is easy to see that there are certain formulas involved with how movies are written, directed, produced, and advertised. We may not realize the formulas as regular movie goers, but the more we think critically about it, the more we can learn to recognize the techniques used to attract us to a particular movie.

ACTIVITY: Movie Marketing

What you need: A group of people who have seen some recent movies.

How long it takes: This exercise takes about 30 minutes or so to complete.

What it teaches: This exercise teaches how word of mouth helps make a movie popular or unpopular, taking into account the movie studio's own promotional campaign.

The activity: Think about a movie that is currently out in theatres and is being considered a big hit - the movie everyone is talking about right now. Consider why the movie is such a big success. Does the movie have big-name celebrities playing the main characters? Is the story supposed to be great? Did the movie get good reviews from the critics? Have you seen a lot of advertising for the movie? Ask someone who has NOT seen the movie why they think the movie is so popular. Then ask someone who HAS seen the movie why it is so popular. Did the person who saw the movie actually like it? Why or why not?

What is going on: Although movie studios spend a great amount of money on advertising a movie, ultimately a movie's success relies on word of mouth advertising – someone telling someone else whether a movie is worth seeing or not. When talking about movie advertising, word of mouth goes beyond just a friend telling another friend about the movie. It includes recommendations from movie critics in newspapers and on television. Word of mouth advertising is so important for movies that movie studios often put out their own commercials in which we hear from people who just got out of the movie and are telling us how great it was. There are many movies in Hollywood that have had large production and advertising budgets, but still flopped because of poor word of mouth review.

ACTIVITY: Appeal

What you need: A group of people who have seen some recent movies.

How long it takes: This exercise takes about 30 minutes or so to complete.

What it teaches: This exercise teaches how to recognize that movies are made for specific people in specific target audiences, and not all movies will appeal to everyone.

The activity: Consider the last movie you saw in theatres or on video. Think about the reasons you liked or did not like the movie. How did the movie try to appeal to you? Did the movie have celebrities in it or did it have little-known actors but a great story? If you liked the movie, would you recommend it to your friends? Would you recommend it to your parents? Why or why not? If you did not like it, why not? Movie producers try to make movies that appeal to a particular audience. Do you think you were the movie's intended audience? Why or why not?

What is going on: Movies are made for specific people in specific target audiences, and so not every movie will likely appeal to you. Movie producers try to give you hints about who the intended audience is when they tell you about the story, the actors and directors involved, and the genre. These elements signal to us whether we might like a particular movie or not. Sometimes, American movie producers try to go outside of the norms and present us with a movie that is slightly different than we expect – maybe it is a romantic comedy where the main characters die (not supposed to happen in American movies), or an action movie where the villain wins (also a no-no in Hollywood) – and we react negatively to these changes since they do not meet our expectations.

Chapter 6 – Music

Today's music industry is fascinating in many ways. Not only has music consumption changed in the last decade, thanks in large part to the internet and downloadable music, but music has become more than simply a form of entertainment – it has become a way to understand popular culture. Today we seem to pay attention to the lives of the artists more than ever before, and we tend to follow their cues when we decide how to dress, how to speak, and how to act around our friends. Popular music has become an important part of how we experience media, from television show theme songs and movie soundtracks, to music used in television and radio advertisements.

The current state of affairs in the music industry is largely a result of websites like YouTube. We no longer need to watch MTV to see our favorite music videos or hear new music. In fact, MTV rarely shows music videos these days. Instead we can point to YouTube and listen to our favorite artist's new hit single for free and at any time we would like. The visual and cultural aspects of music now dominate our eyes and minds as well as our ears. As a result, it is more difficult than ever for popular artists to stand out among a sea of musicians involved in a somewhat level playing field. The music industry has become democratic in some respects – anyone can create a music video and post it on YouTube, and anyone can record their album using home recording equipment and release it on iTunes. Music directors – the people who choose music for television and movies – source their music from both major artists and from independent musicians without a record label deal. The standout performers do have the financial backing of record labels, which helps give them more exposure, but only because the label thinks an artist can make a lot of money for them.

So more and more, the popular music industry is tasked with convincing the audience to appreciate what they see and feel and less and less about what they hear. Sure, a song still needs to be appealing to the listener when they hear it on the radio. But knowing who the song was made by is as important as what the song sounds like. This new holistic approach to the musical product is how we approach music from a media literacy perspective. We are not just interested in what a song sounds like, but what does the song mean? How does it affect the way we dress and the words we use? How does the entire musical product (the song, the video, the artist) affect the way we behave? These are the questions we want to ask ourselves as we study music and its effects on our lives.

Musical Genres

We can begin our discussion of music by defining some common genres, or categories, of music. These genres will tell us a lot about how the music and the musicians fit with their audiences. Genres can tell us everything from what kind of instruments are acceptable in the genre, to what themes are represented in the music. A musical genre can also clue us in to who the audience is for a particular song.

Take for example rock music; can you define what elements are used to construct a rock song? You might find that most rock songs feature a guitar of some sort – maybe acoustic, but likely electric. Rock songs also typically have recurring themes, with one major theme being growing up as a middle-class teenager who is discontent with society. Another element of rock music that we typically encounter is that the vocalist is typically male. When you watch rock videos on YouTube, are there any elements, objects, types of clothing, or stories that are common among them? A common rock stereotype is the long-haired, tattooed rocker wearing all black. When we combine all of these elements, we will find that most rock songs and music videos have a similar feel and they appeal to a specific audience – mostly young males.

Another genre we can discuss is hip-hop. What elements define a typical hip-hop song? Typically, we hear a slower electronic beat as the main element of the soundtrack. One common theme in hip-hop is growing up in difficult situations, and finding ways to overcome life's obstacles. We may hear both men and women singing in hip-hop songs. A common stereotype we see in hip-hop videos is expensive vehicles, female dancers, and over-the-top scenes or situations. When we combine these elements, we will find that most hip-hop songs and music videos, just like with most rock songs and music videos, have a similar feel and they appeal to a specific audience – mostly young males and females.

Think about other genres of music you may have heard, and think critically about the elements that help define those genres. What make jazz music (and the "jazz scene") different than country music (and the "country scene")? Is house music at all like swing music? By asking these questions and digging deeper into the elements of a song or musician, we can better understand the similarities and differences among all of these types of music.

Sound Literacy

An important aspect of understanding the way music works – and why certain songs or pieces of music might make us feel a certain way – is understanding the socially-accepted meanings of certain musical elements.

Here is an example of this concept. What emotions come to mind if I told you that a piece of music has a slow beat, is played in minor chords, and the vocalist sings with what seems like very low energy? You are probably thinking 'sad' or 'lethargic'. How about if I said the music is very fast tempo, uses major chords, has a very animated vocalist singing with enthusiasm? In this case, you're probably thinking 'happy' or 'excited'. I never mentioned what the lyrics were about or what genre these two very different songs are from. But we have accepted, as a society, to agree that the first song means 'sad' and the second song means 'happy'. This natural intuition may have been learned in childhood, when we watched movies like the *Lion King*, and heard sad music play as sad things happen on the screen. Our brains have made the connections over time and through repeated exposure, and now we can sense a piece of music's emotional content by just listening.

The exercises that follow will help you better understand how to interpret music by analyzing different components of a song, determining the genre and audience of a piece of music or artist, and evaluating music marketing as a way to appeal to us.

ACTIVITY: Genre

What you need: A piece of music by any artist.

How long it takes: This exercise takes approximately 20 minutes to complete.

What it teaches: The genre, or category, of a song is made up of various elements in the song. This exercise teaches how to recognize a song's genre, and why genres exist.

The activity: Listen to a piece of music and think about what genre, or category, it belongs to. Is the song, rock, rap, hip hop, jazz, country, classical, or something else? Think about how you arrived at your answer. What elements of the song tell you what genre the music belongs to? Some genres are associated with certain elements like the instruments used in the song, the singer's tone of voice, the song's length, and the tempo. Which of these elements indicated that this song belongs in the genre you chose? Why does the piece of music fit into the genre you chose and not another? Would the song still belong in the genre if the singer was of a different race, age, or gender? Why did you choose this song to analyze? How did it appeal to you?

What is going on: Musical pieces fit within a particular genre by following certain guidelines belonging to that genre. For example, classical music is characterized by the use of classical instruments like violin and flute, the absence of a singer, the length of the composition (generally anywhere from 6 to 20 minutes), and the audience that it appeals to (generally people older than 40 years old). The genre can tell you a lot about the piece's audience as well. A classic rock song might appeal to one group of people, while a current pop song might appeal to a completely different group of people. Genres use conventions that meet the audience's expectations. You expect electric guitar in a rock song. You expect a slower tempo for a song in the Blues genre. Imagine a rock song in which the guitar is replaced by a flute, or a classical piece with a singer yelling at the top of his voice. These examples break genre conventions, so they either do not exist or they are highly unpopular. Musical genres help the audience decide what to listen to by giving them a name for common characteristics across a variety of pieces. Someone who typically enjoys Bluegrass music has certain expectations of the music they listen to, so they expect few surprises when they buy a new album labeled as "Bluegrass."

ACTIVITY: Lyrics

What you need: A piece of music with lyrics by any artist.

How long it takes: This exercise takes approximately 30 minutes to complete.

What it teaches: This exercise teaches how to interpret the meaning of song's lyrics, and examine what types of emotions lyrics can invoke in the listener.

The activity: Listen to a piece of music with lyrics and think about the way the lyrics make you feel. What types of emotions do the lyrics make you experience? Do they make you feel happy? Sad? Angry? Does the emotional feeling the lyrics convey match with the way the singer sings those lyrics? For example, if the lyrics convey happiness, does the singer sound happy? Does the music fit with the lyrics and singing, or is there a disconnect? For example, maybe the lyrics and singing sound sad, but the song is still up tempo. How do the actual lyrics and their message make you feel? Is there a story being told through lyrics, and can you relate to that story? How are the lyrics written to appeal to the song's audience? Try writing new lyrics for the song and give them the opposite meaning. Does the song still work?

What is going on: Lyrics are an integral part of today's popular music. They are written to appeal to the audience, and they carry a message the audience can relate to. Sometimes, the lyrics make the audience feel a certain way that does not follow the feeling that the music provides.

ACTIVITY: Instrumentation and Song Structure

What you need: A current "hit" song by any artist, as well as a "hit" song from 20 or 30 years ago.

How long it takes: This exercise takes approximately 30 minutes to complete.

What it teaches: This exercise teaches how to listen to the instruments in a song as a way to understand the song's message. Songs follow a particular structure that help them be memorable with their audience.

The activity: Listen to a song that is either constantly played on the radio or that is currently popular on YouTube. Take note of the types of instruments used in the song and how those instruments contribute to the song's overall feeling. Also take note of the song's structure – does the song start with a catchy phrase or musical notes, or maybe does it constantly repeat catchy "hooks" over and over again? Consider how these repeating sections make you feel. Does the song get "stuck in your head?" Why do you think this happens? How does the song's arrangement – the way the instruments play together – make you feel? Does it make you want to dance, or does it almost put you to sleep? Does the arrangement make you feel happy or sad? Does it make you feel cool? Why or why not? Why do you think this song is so popular on the radio or on YouTube? Is it the music, the singer, the culture associated with the song, or something else?

Does how your friends feel about this song affect how you feel about it? Now listen to a song in the same genre but that is 20 or 30 years old. Does this song make you feel the same way as the first song? Why or why not? What has changed in the production style, instrumentation, and arrangement over that time? Why did those changes occur?

What is going on: Current popular music tends to follow a formula to help make a song "catchy", which in turn helps increase its popularity. A song's production style and arrangement conveys a lot of meaning – who a song is targeted to, what the song's message is, what the genre is, etc. Today's music is finely tuned for commercial success, more so than it was 20 or 30 years ago. Understanding why a song appeals to us, whether it is the music or something else, helps us better understand our relationship with the music and with popular culture. Sometimes the music itself has little to do with if we like a song or not – the song could appeal to us culturally if we have friends that like it or if it is associated with a particular event or emotion.

ACTIVITY: Target Audience

What you need: A piece of music by any artist.

How long it takes: This exercise takes approximately 30 minutes to complete.

What it teaches: This exercise teaches how to recognize the target audience for a particular song. There are many clues associated with the song that will help us determine this.

The activity: Listen to a piece of music from any genre. Now consider who the song's intended target audience (ideal target audience) is? What values do the lyrics contain? Does the way in which the artist portrays him or herself affect how you feel about the song? Would you feel the same way about the song if someone of a different age, race, or gender sang it? How might someone different than you interpret the song? What message does the song send? Is the message positive or negative?

What is going on: You can tell a lot about a song's target audience just by listening to it. Specific genres generally try to appeal to a particular ideal target market. This can be seen in how radio stations target their audiences based on music. Radio stations that play Modern Rock, for example, target white male teens more than any other group. This means that for a song on that station to gain in popularity, the musician tries to cater the lyrics, music, and the lifestyle they portray to the young people in that target audience. This is one reason you see the grown men and women in these bands dressed like teenagers! They are trying to appeal to their target market.

ACTIVITY: Music Marketing

What you need: Drawing paper and a pen or pencil for each participant in this exercise.

How long it takes: This exercise could take up to an hour or more, depending on how much time is given for drawing, and how much time is given for the presentation of the final works.

What it teaches: This exercise helps participants understand how music is sold to its intended target market through one of many techniques – album cover design.

The activity: Design an album cover for a new fictional album for your favorite band or musician. Take into account the band or musician's genre, the lifestyle they convey, and the target audience that the album is aimed towards. Explain why they are your favorite band or musician, and why others might like them. Explain why you believe the album cover you created would help sell this new album to the target market.

What is going on: Although the online music video has become the most important marketing piece for any musician or band trying to gain popular approval, the album cover is still one of the most important ways we relate to an artist, especially over the long term. The album cover says a lot about the musician's "brand" and it helps the audience recognize the album in a store or in their music library. So an album's cover needs to convey a message telling the listener what to expect from the music and the lifestyle associated with it. This is why many dance albums have images of people dancing and having a good time on them. Rock albums often have ironic or thought provoking covers, indicating a depth in the music and in the artistic effort. Country albums, typically focusing on the singer/songwriter, have images of the lead singer or people in the band. Album covers follow conventions, often dictated by genre, that are meant to appeal to the target audience.

Chapter 7 – News Media

News is all around us. It is one of the only types of media that is an actual type of message that can freely be adapted to various media formats (advertising is another). In other words, news can be read online, heard on the radio, seen on TV, read in newspapers or magazines, and even be spread by word of mouth.

But what exactly is news, and what makes a particular event news or "newsworthy"? Is it news whern something happens and it gets reported on? What if something important happens but it doesn't get reported on in a newspaper – is that news? Well, keep in mind that what may be important to you may not be that important to me. So how do the people who write the news choose what stories to use as "news"? Yes, news is created by someone. It does not just pop out of no where and just appear online, in print, or from the lips of your local TV newscaster. Someone actually says "this is what we will choose as our headline today" and "this is news and this is not". If you and I ran competing news websites in a town or city, the story I choose as the most important story (and thereby make it my main headline) might be different than the top headline and story you choose. We see the world differently, and so different things are important to us.

Why does news even exist? Do we even need news? Can we do without news? Let us explore news a little more.

What is news?

The best place to begin is with a working definition of news. News can mean different things to different people, but the simplest way we an explain in for our purposes is to say that news is ***an event reported on in the media***. This definition is broad and perhaps unsatisfying, but there is a lot of room to expand from that basic definition.

Let us think about what this defiition of news implies. Have you ever hear the saying, “if a tree falls in the forest and no one is around to hear it, does it really make a sound?” The same can be said about news. If a car crash happes on your street, but it is not reported on in any news outlet, is it really news? It’s possible that the story of the crash is newsworthy, meaning it could be interesting enough to be considered news, but that is different from actual news. For example, suppose that your city's mayor was involved in the car crash on your street. People might want to know about this, so the event is considered to be newsworthy. But then suppose that nobody got hurt in the car accident, and the mayor exchanged insurance with the other driver and they both left the scene. In this case, no police were called, no reporters wrote any stories, and no photographers took any pictures. The event was quick and was only experineced by those two participants. In this case, because the event did not appear in any news outlets, this is not news, though it may still be newsworthy.

In this section we will make a distinction between **news** and **newsworthy**, with the former being an event reported on in the media, and the latter as something that deserves to be in the news.

So what does it mean for something to be newsworthy? Newsworthy typically means out of the ordinary. The classic example says, if dog bites man, that is not news. However, if man bites dog, that is news. The former happens often, and the latter rarely if ever happens. The fact that for something to be newsworthy it needs to be out of the oridnary is a very important media literacy concept to grasp. If this is true, that means that what we read in the news is not a regular occurance in society. Consider how this fact affects how news helps shape our world.

If you have ever watched an evening television newscast, you have probably realized that their top stories – the stories they talk about at the very beginning of the broadcast – are tyically about bad things that have happened in the city. Perhaps they will lead with news of a murder, a kidnapping, or some other violent crime. Remember, the news media show us things that are out of the ordinary. But if we constantly see the same sad stories of murder and other violence in the news, we will begin to believe that the world is a very dangerous place – at least more dagerous than it actually is. In fact, we need to remember that these news stories are showing us things happening in the world that are not common.

Another aspect of news is that, believe it or not, news is supposed to be entertaining to read or watch. Take the sports report as an example. It would be very boring to simply show the final score of a baseball game in a newspaper.

The Dodgers beat the Mariners 5-4.

Imagine if that was the entire report. There are many things wrong with this. First of all, the report is short. Newspapers and online news outlets like the *Huffington Post* make much of there money from selling advertising in their pages, so it is to their advantage to publish longer stories to keep you turning pages or clicking "*next*" and looking at more ads. But more importantly, showing the score this way is very boring and not at all unique. If there are two or three newspapers in town (or hundreds of sports websites online) where you can find the same score, what makes this unique? Why would anyone buy your newspaper, or watch your newscast, or visit your website? This fact makes it important for news to be entertaining in addition to being informing. So instead of just the sports score, you're likely to read or see an entire report about the game, with summaries by inning, stand out players, the game's best plays, and commentary about what the teams did right and what went wrong. This makes the report unique, interesting, and entertaining. However, "unique, interesting, and entertaining" also means that the news is not always objecive and could have some bias.

Bias in News

Bias in news occurs when a journalist interjects her/his personal point of view or perception of a newsworthy event. An example may be in a local newspaper's reporting of a baseball game and they intentionally focus on the home team rather than on the visiting team. Another obvious example is in political reporting and the reporter obviously favors one politician over another. Journalists are taught to avoid bias news reporting when possible.

While eliminating bias in news reporting is an admirable goal, it is actaully impossible to remove all bias in news stories. You may think that if the journalist only presents the facts without writing about their own opinion, this is enough to write news that is free of bias. This is a mistake – by the very fact that journalists are writing about this story and not something else, they are introducing bias.

An example of this, which may not be obvious at first, is when The Wall Street Journal (WSJ), a politically conservative-leaning newspaper, writes a story about President Obama, who leans liberal. The newspaper may print only the facts about news related to

President Obama, but they may only choose stories about failures for the president and leave out stories about his successes. The newspaper is introducing bias with the simple act of choosing which stories to include in the paper!

Another example of this type of bias is in the sports section of the newspaper. Have you ever noticed which sports your local newspaper or news show decides to focus on, and which they choose to minimize or exclude? For example, in the Los Angeles Times sports section they tend to prominently cover the following professional men's sports: baseball, basketball, football, hockey, and golf. However, sports like Formula 1, professional women's basketball, and any women's college sports are rarely if ever covered. This may be due to the audience's interest in those pro sports, but it is still a bias of which to be aware.

There are a few places in news that bias is expected and even encouraged – in editorials and opinion pieces, and in columns. Editorials are written by the editorial staff to give then an opportunity to share their thoughts on a topic. Opinion pieces are often written by contributors who do not typically write for the newspaper and who have an opinion on a particular issue. Columns are written by special repor6ters called columnists – their job is to write their (often controversial) opinion on a hot topic in the news. When reading newspapers or watching your local or network news broadcast, be aware of what type of news story you are experiencing. Is the story based on facts or opinion? How can you tell the diference?

Reporters at the New York Times research and write news stories for tomorrow's paper.

http://loc.gov/pictures/resource/cph.3c12969/

What types of elements make up a news story? Whenever you read a news story or watch a newscast you will notice that the story tries to answer the following six questions about the event: **who, what, when, where, why, how**. Any well written news story will include the answers to these questions. Let us look at each in turn.

- **Who** – Who is the story about? This includes the person's name, role in the story, and why we should care about this particular person.
- **What** – What is this story about? Here we want to know what happened and why it is important that we know about it.
- **When** – When did this event happen? This usually includes the date and time for events that occurred in the past 24 hours.
- **Where** – Where did this event happen? If this is a local news story, it may include an address or the closest intersection.
- **Why** – Why did this event happen? What circumstances lead to this event?
- **How** – How did this event happen? This is a detailed description of the event as it unfolded.

Here is an example “news story” that we can analyze using these six questions. This fun example is not only an example of the elements of a news story, but it also illustrates bias in news, newsworthiness, and considering your audience when choosing a point of view.

Once upon a time, there was a little girl named Goldilocks. She went for a walk in the forest. Pretty soon, she came upon a house. She knocked and, when no one answered, she walked right in. At the table in the kitchen, there were three bowls of porridge. Goldilocks was hungry. She tasted the porridge from the first bowl.

"This porridge is too hot!" she exclaimed.

So, she tasted the porridge from the second bowl.

"This porridge is too cold," she said

So, she tasted the last bowl of porridge.

"Ahhh, this porridge is just right," she said happily and she ate it all up.

After she'd eaten the three bears' breakfasts she decided she was feeling a little tired. So, she walked into the living room where she saw three chairs. Goldilocks sat in the first chair to rest her feet.

"This chair is too big!" she exclaimed.

So she sat in the second chair.

"This chair is too big, too!" she whined.

So she tried the last and smallest chair.

"Ahhh, this chair is just right," she sighed. But just as she settled down into the chair to rest, it broke into pieces!

Goldilocks was very tired by this time, so she went upstairs to the bedroom. She lay down in the first bed, but it was too hard. Then she lay in the second bed, but it was too soft. Then she lay down in the third bed and it was just right. Goldilocks fell asleep.

As she was sleeping, the three bears came home.

"Someone's been eating my porridge," growled the Papa bear.

"Someone's been eating my porridge," said the Mama bear.

"Someone's been eating my porridge and they ate it all up!" cried the Baby bear.

"Someone's been sitting in my chair," growled the Papa bear.

"Someone's been sitting in my chair," said the Mama bear.

"Someone's been sitting in my chair and they've broken it all to pieces," cried the Baby bear.

They decided to look around some more and when they got upstairs to the bedroom, Papa bear growled, "Someone's been sleeping in my bed,"

"Someone's been sleeping in my bed, too" said the Mama bear

"Someone's been sleeping in my bed and she's still there!" exclaimed Baby bear.

Just then, Goldilocks woke up and saw the three bears. She screamed, "Help!" And she jumped up and ran out of the room. Goldilocks ran down the stairs, opened the door, and ran away into the forest. And she never returned to the home of the three bears.

You will recognize this story as Goldilocks and the Three Bears. Let us analyze the story from Goldilocks' perspective.

Goldilocks and the Three Bears – From the perspective of Goldilocks

- Who – Goldilocks.

- What – She finds a home in the forest, has some porridge, takes a nap, and is frightened by a family of bears.
- When – Once upon a time, of course!
- Where – The forest.
- Why – She was walking through the forest and was curious.
- How – She went right into the house (the door was unlocked), she saw three porridges and tried one at a time, etc. etc.

If this story was to appear in the human newspaper, the headline might read, "Girl walks through the forest, attacked by three bears." However, things change if we look at it from the three bears' perspective!

Goldilocks and the Three Bears – From the perspective of the Three Bears

- Who – The three bears.
- What – The three bears come home to discover that their home has been burglarized, with the burger eating their food and sleeping in their beds.
- When – Once upon a time.

- Where – The forest.
- Why – The bears left their front door unlocked, the burglar was hungry and tired.
- How – The three bears arrive home, they see a mess at their table, they notice their furniture had been moved, and they discover the girl sleeping in one of the beds.

As you can see, this same story has a different meaning when analyzed from the perspective of the three bears. If this story appeared in the Daily Bear Gazette, the headline might read, "Frightened bear family victimized by human, assailant still at large."

Today's news media is saturated by a variety of sources, some more legitimate than others. This world we live in, with the addition of social media, internet anonymity, the reader-as-creator model, the sheer plentitude of media outlets (both commercial and not), the world is a much different place.

Here are some things to be aware of when consuming news, especially news that you found through social media.

Click bait

If you have ever wanted to quickly click on a headline on Facebook, out of sheer curiosity and perhaps even instinct, then you have experienced click bait. Sometimes, the headline relates to something you are interested in, but most of the time the headline simply appeals to our base instincts – love, hate, fear, sex, wonder or curiosity, challenge, amazement, shock, or greed. Usually the headline's subject is not something we would normally click on, but for some reason we felt compelled to click on this particular headline. Most of the time we are disappointed after clicking, the headline leading to a story that is underwhelming and that does not live up to the headline's hype. The goal of click bait is to get the reader to click through to the full article, helping to lift their viewer counts and perhaps earn advertising revenue.

Here are some example click bait headlines:

Man Tries to Hug a Wild Lion, You Won't Believe What Happens Next!

A School Girl Gave Her Lunch To A Homeless Man. What He Did Next Will Leave You In Tears

21 Stars Who Ruined Their Face Due To Plastic Surgery. Talk About Regrets!

Man Divorced His Wife After Knowing What Is In This Photo

Can You Solve This Ancient Riddle? 90% People Gave The Wrong Answer

Supermodels Apply These Three Simple Trick To Look Young

Girls Won't Be Able To Resist If You Apply This Simple Trick

Is Your Boyfriend Cheating On You? He Is, If He Does These Five Things

9 Things No One Knew About Princess Leia. Number 7 Will Blow Your Minds

Fake News

"Fake news is a type of yellow journalism or propaganda that consists of deliberate misinformation or hoaxes spread via traditional print and broadcast news media or online social media. Fake news is written and published with the intent to mislead in order to damage an agency, entity, or person, and/or gain financially or politically, often using sensationalist, dishonest, or outright fabricated headlines to increase readership, online sharing, and Internet click revenue. In the latter case, it is similar to sensational online "clickbait" headlines and relies on advertising revenue generated from this activity, regardless of the veracity of the published stories. Intentionally misleading and deceptive fake news is different from obvious satire or parody, which is intended to humor rather than mislead its audience."
– Wikipedia

Fake news has been around for a very long time. We might see it today at the checkout stand at the supermarket as tabloid magazines that claim that aliens have abducted the American president. Most of us know better than to believe that these stories are true, but the news is presented as if it were true. The earliest version of this on the internet is from the satirical website, The Onion. The Onion originated in the 1990s, and its goal has always been to lampoon the news by writing stories that are just so believable that you need to give it a second read to be sure. They make no fuss about the fact that their news stories are fake, although some real news stories often sound more outlandish than even the writers at The Onion could devise.

When we talk about fake news in today's world, we are really talking about the news that presents itself as credible, though it contains factual inaccuracies or is outright misleading. Often, we may label fake news as such because of an inaccurate headline or due to incorrect information in the story itself. An example is when President Trump has made a claim to have never made so-and-so a statement, but there is actual video of him having made that statement. The president is trying to dissuade criticism by calling the coverage of this incident as fake news.

The problem here is not usually with the mainstream media, since most corporate-owned mass media outlets attempt to fact check news and information before printing or airing it. The problem lies with small “$2 news start-ups” that are run by amateur journalists (or foreign governments) that have little regard for the truth, and they end up disseminating the information to their audience, who either believes the information is correct, or fails to fact check it themselves. This spread of fake news has increased in recent years with the rise of social media services like Twitter and private messaging programs like Whatsapp. Information spreads so quickly these days, and often we barely have time to think about a particular media message’s authenticity before receiving the next notification.

Fake news can be defeated if media consumers began using media literacy and media criticism techniques to filter out inaccurate and incorrect information. This is a tall ask, one that is not likely to be adopted by the majority of the public. Recognizing that information could be untrue is a good first step in fighting against false information. The critical thinking skills taught in this book should help, though more people need to be aware of them in order for them to become effective in disabling the negative impact on our democracy.

Yellow Journalism

Yellow journalism could be categorized as journalism that plays loose with the facts, favors sensationalizing facts and spreading rumors rather than providing useful information, and putting profits over credibility. Some of the types of media we explore here can be considered a part of yellow journalism, especially fake news and click bait, but more so, yellow journalism finds its way in all types of commercial media for the simple fact that commercial media are businesses, and thus are most interested in profits.

Yellow journalism finds its origins in the early 1900s with the newspapers of William Randolph Hearst, as popularized by the movie, Citizen Kane. Hearst newspapers were known to include sensational headlines and cover photos, incomplete or false information, and with sales as its main goal. As Charles Foster Kane said in the movie, "[people will think] what I want them to think."

Today, yellow journalism in print survives in the form of supermarket tabloids like The National Enquirer and Star magazines. These magazines literally concern themselves with the gossip of housewives, as Citizen Kane predicted, along with astrology readings, mean-spirited and often aggressive takes on celebrity news, and salacious headlines meant to grab attention and produce sales.

Forms of Yellow journalism also survive in non-print media today, and its hallmarks can be experienced in most forms of commercial media. I prime example is the "breaking news" alert, a once rarely used advisory to let people know that what they are about to see if new and just in, is used for nearly every news story in order to gain the audience's attention and keep them tuned in.

During the 2016 primaries and then general elections, the broadcast and cable media were obsessed with Donald Trump's candidacy for president, cutting away from normal programming to bring the "breaking news" of another Donald Trump campaign rally. The media knew that Donald Trump was likely to say something sensational or outlandish, and they wanted to show it live, believing that their audience would want to watch it (and presumably change the channel to another outlet if the current channel did not air it). It has been reported by The New York Times that Donald Trump received $2 billion of free media publicity in this way.

If we examine the media's incessant desire to lean towards the sensational and extraordinary in their reporting, it is only fair that we discuss the audience's own desires to consume such content as a reason why we experience certain subjects in the first place. Since we know that the media are businesses, and that the main motivation for a business is to make a profit, it can be argued that commercial media uses sensationalism because it makes greater profits by giving us, the audience, what we want.

In other words, if we were not so interested in Donald Trump and the next thing he was going to say, the media would not carry his campaign rallies live. After all, the television networks have access to audience viewing data, and they could see that their ratings would rise when Donald Trump was on the air. Of course, an argument could be made that the media should bring us, not just the information we want but the information we need. However, in an era of intense media competition for viewers, it is difficult to justify showing us anything by which we are at all challenged.

Yellow journalism will continue to exist until, we as an audience, decide we have had enough of the sensational, superficial, biased news media that feeds our current information addiction. Until we demand more in depth coverage of a wider array of topics, we will continue to see the same types of stories in commercial news media. Alternative media, characterized as such due to its funding model (non-profit, government or viewer funded), includes public broadcasters PBS and NPR, and less-than-commercial newspapers like The Guardian. While still biased toward a certain point of view, these news media outlets tend to be far less sensational and focus on a wide array of news topics.

The Echo Chamber

The Echo chamber is a place we put ourselves in as members of an audience where the same information bounces around to us from different directions, effectively making it seem like everyone is saying the same things. An example is when Donald Trump won the 2016 presidential election, Democrats and people on the left who expected Hillary Clinton to win were flabbergasted. How could they not have seen that coming? The answer is echo chambers.

People expecting a Clinton win watched the same news shows, which featured guests from the same newspapers, and they featured the same experts giving the same polling data. Democrats were in the echo chamber. Everyone seemed to be saying the same thing – that Trump was going to lose and Clinton would win in a big way. The problem was that outside of the echo chamber, other information was being disseminated that people inside of it were not aware of. This is another reason that we should consume news and information from a variety of sources and not from just a few.

You may have heard of how the so-called algorithm is in control of the information we see online. This algorithm is just an online version of the echo chamber meant to limit our exposure to a wide variety of news and information in order to get us dialed in to viewing more and more content we agree with. Here is an imaginary monologue by YouTube's algorithm: "This person enjoys farming videos? Let's show them only farming videos – this way they will see what they enjoy, are more likely to watch for longer, and will likely not be upset because we are not challenging them in any way. More viewership means they will see more ads." I personally prefer to be challenged and to see things I am not used to seeing. This is why every few weeks I clear out my YouTube history so I stop receiving the same few recommended videos to watch.

Unfortunately, there is no way that I am aware of to turn off this recommendation algorithm, but I know it exists all over the internet; on Amazon, on Google, and on news sites. These websites fine tune the products and information they show us to maximize profit. Again, there is nothing we can do but be aware that this is happening and be vigilant of the things being presented to us.

The $2 news startup

When I first launched my media website, *UnderstandMedia.com* back in the early 2000s, all I had was a domain name that cost me $1.99, and a free web hosting service. With just $2, I was able to create a website from which I could present my ideas and share my views with the world. At the time, I was a young academic with lots of ideas and a great deal of ambition. However, there was no one around that I needed to gain permission from in order to publish to my site. I had complete control over the content and the direction of the site.

One of the biggest ironies of social media and the open internet is that sites like mine could exists next to websites with nefarious goals. The model with which I launched my website could be used by someone wanting to launch their own news site, without the need for a degree of journalism or even working knowledge of how journalism works, including the aspects related to ethics and integrity. Anyone, even you, could launch your own news site today for $2.

The good news is that the open internet and social media have helped democratize information to some degree. While it is true that not everyone with a $2 website will become the next media or news sensation, the fact is that everyone has the potential to be if they work hard enough. While some have worked hard on building a reputation for accurate reporting (many even winning awards for journalism), many have worked hard at spreading misinformation. In a way, the advent of the $2 news start-up was a backlash of the corporate-controlled media that disallowed audience participation. The pendulum has swung to the opposite end of the spectrum, with anyone now able to create a message and send it out into the world.

This makes the case for why we need to be critical of all of the news we consume, and to verify the source when possible. A good rule of thumb for verifying a news story from a $2 news start-up is to try finding the story on another, perhaps more reputable news site. If for example, if XYZ News published a story and you are able to find that story on CNN as well, that means CNN has validated the key facts and have determined that they are correct (often they will state when they cannot or have not validated the facts). In the old days of news, a scoop or exclusive news story was worth its weight in gold, but today an exclusive story could be s form of deception unless otherwise validated.

While you may think that avoiding news from $2 news start-ups is simple enough – only read news from trusted news sources or only use a service like Google News or Apple News to find stories. In the first case, you may be correct – if you only get your news from the Washington Post, The New York Times, or the Wall Street Journal, you are likely to be reading reputable (though biased) news coverage, but you are limiting your sphere of knowledge and then you enter the echo chamber – the same ideas bounce off from similar circles of information. To avoid this, you may use Google News to broaden your horizons or tune in to TYT on YouTube for a different perspective. Just know that Google News may syndicate news stories from $2 news start-ups, so you are not guaranteed accurate news.

Persuasion tactics

The news media uses many tactics to persuade us to their point of view. Remember, all media is bias to some degree, whether wittingly or unwittingly. The three main cable news networks, CNN, MSNBC, and Fox News, many times display their bias forcefully and with obvious knowledge that they are doing so. This may sometimes come directly from the news anchor, presenting opinion as fact, blatantly supporting and illustrating one side of an issue.

The talking head

The talking head is a common tactic used in television news in order to provide support for a point of view. The talk head is the guest to the show who is in a box, calling in from somewhere, to deliver their point of view. Typically, the news anchor sets up the story, perhaps mixes fact with opinion, and then says "for more on this, let's bring in our correspondent..." and the correspondent appears in a box. On the screen. This technique was used long before the pandemic, when guests could go on a show and be there in person, but now having a talking head (but usually several) is the norm. In this case, the anchor serves more as a moderator than provider of truth.

The talking head's job is to reinforce what the anchor is discussing. For example, during the pandemic, MSNBC wanted to show just how badly President Trump was doing at working through the pandemic. The anchor gave a short report, and then brought in a medical doctor, a political correspondent, and a reporter from the News York Times or the Washington Post who had written a recent story about the topic. The newscaster, along with the talking heads, each with a different angle on the story, combined to give the audience a particular perspective and version of the truth.

Sometimes, talking heads are not friendly "contributors," but instead they are hostile subjects from the opposite side of an issue. In this case, the news anchor asks questions they don't know the answer to, and they are trying to combat against the guest to reach the truth of the matter. The following are some ways hostile guests try to steer the audience towards a particular narrative.

Spin

Spin is usually used by someone who is defending wrong-doing or a poor outcome to change the negative into a positive or to otherwise detract from the bad news. A classic example of this is when people from the Trump administration went on television to spin bad news. The anchor would say something like "Coronavirus cases are up. It seems like a disaster for the president," to which the talking head (some spokesperson sent to spin the story) would respond, "Well, there's more testing so of course there will be more cases. We're the ones doing the testing. Our plan is working perfectly." By using a slip in logic, the spokesperson can convince some people that what they say is true, but we know this is just spin.

Changing the subject

When hostile guests are caught in an argument they cannot win, often they will attempt to change the subject, trying to spin another piece of news to distract from the main point. They will also use *Whataboutism*, a technique discussed later but which essentially turns the table on the interviewer by asking "Well, what about this that my opponent did..." Changing the subject helps to avoid answering the question by not only not addressing the main point, but by trying to change the main point. During the first two years of President Trump's tenure in office, he would often change the subject by attempting to shift the blame from himself to former President Obama.

Attacking the interviewer

Attacking the interviewer for "being bias," being unfair," or "asking stupid questions" is a technique we see often in the media. The person being interviewed is clearly out of options for responses, so they resort to attacking the person doing the interview, or, at a press conference, the person asking the question. They may also call it "shameful" that such a question be asked, or "how dare you" ask this question. Attacking the interviewer is not very effective at convincing the audience that the guest is being forthright, but the guest's supporters usually appreciate the pushback that the guest presents.

Attacking the media

If all else fails, the guest or interviewee resorts to attacking the media itself. We know that such a blanket statement is stereotypical, and the world is not black and white, but nuanced. But when a public figure wants ignore or discredit outside criticism, they will attack the media itself for bias, lying, profiteering, fake news, and any other number of insults that cannot hold up to scrutiny. Are there some media outlets or newscasters or reporters that deserve being told "your outlet is fake news"? Perhaps, but using a blanket statement is dishonest at best, and damaging to media as an institution at worst.

One important thing that all talking heads, especially hostile guests know, is that everything on television news is timed. Hence, if they find themselves in a heated exchange they are not likely to win, they wait out the clock. This means they use one of the four techniques above until the anchor says "Well, we're out of time..." This is how hostile guests end up not giving any substantive answers during an interview, though of course they will say they proudly went on a particular show and did well during their interview.

The enticing headline

The news media often uses enticing headlines in order to get viewers or get people to click on a link.

The extreme example is click-bait, but more subtle headlines can be enticing but may not be as blatantly obvious as click-bait. An example in cable television news is the constant use of the graphic stating that something is "breaking news." Breaking news used to be a term attached to a story that was just being reported on right that moment, it was new, exciting, important, and the audience should pay attention to it. Today, "breaking news" has lost almost all its power as a way to keep people interested, since it is used on every story. In fact, some networks put the words breaking news in front of every story they run, so whenever you turn to their channel, the words are always visible.

To a lesser extent, online news media typically uses enticing headlines in order to get attention, but these are also more subtle and less subversive than click-bait. An example is during the pandemic, the New York Times would sometimes print headlines like "new record deaths," making the death count seem terrible, and the headline something enticing that readers would want to click on. Whenever something is a record, especially deaths, the audience responds with clicks.

The provocative photo

Online news media can use provocative photos in order to get attention. Photographers typically take many photos of an event, then selecting the best one in order to present a consistent narrative with the written story. As an example, if there was an event with President Trump, and the story had to do with his poll numbers going down, the photo that is selected to go along with the article might show him hanging his head, or perhaps being caught with a frown. A quarter of a second is all that is needed in order to take a picture that shows a frown from one that shows a smile.

The next time you watch a news conference, listen for the clicks in the background. These are camera shutters going off at precise moments when the speaker says something important or relevant. It is always amusing when the speaker does something simple like raise their hand, and suddenly all you hear is cameras clicking. Photographers want to take relevant photos, but they also want to take photos that provoke an emotion in the reader.

The denial

Public figures will often deny an allegation at first, perhaps believing there is no evidence for the allegation. After all, whatever they say on television or online can come back to haunt them later, so it is always best to start with a denial. This is what many public figures believe, yet the news media is often very good at seeking facts about a case, and they will eventually print the truth if it is discovered that a public figure denied an allegation and then were caught lying.

The straight out lie

The straight out lie is different than a denial in that the straight out lie can be verified immediately as a lie, whereas a denial may stay as such if there is no evidence to judge either way. President Trump has been known to say "I never said that," followed by a video of him saying whatever he denied. Many liberals thought, "Why would he say he didn't say that if he did. It's right there in the video!" Well, the more you say something, and the more you hear it from your candidate, the more you will believe it is true. Or in the case with President Trump, his followers were elated with every denial, fired up that he was so smoothly rejecting an obvious truth.

The statistic

If you have ever studied statistics, you know that statistical results can be manipulated in order to weaken or reinforce a particular point of view. Many people do not even bother with what a statistic means. They see numbers on the screen, and immediately think that the news media knows what they are doing, so "who am I to question it?"

During the pandemic, the New York Times would print statistics about how many new infections were reported the previous day, along with how many deaths. Since I read it every day for personal interest in current events, I noticed there were some days they did not publish the new infections at the top center of the page, and it turns out these were days when new infection records were not set, so perhaps the editor thought it was not as important to publish that statistic. They often also changed the averages (7-day average, 14-day average) and changed the scale of their graphs to make things look worse than they were. The main narrative of the New York Times was that President Trump was doing an awful job handling the coronavirus, so this manipulation of statistics fit perfectly with their broader narrative.

Now that you know a bit more about how the news media work, try some of the following activities to practice your news media literacy skills.

The Trump effect

Live coverage

President Trump enjoys being on camera, and during the pandemic, which coincided with the 2020 presidential campaign, he knew he could draw a large audience on live television. This live audience watched him on live television because they wanted to hear what he had to say, whether they liked him or not. During the 2016 election campaign, 24-hour cable news networks took his rallies live, believing they would garner high ratings, paying little attention to the fact that his rallies were filled with sensational, false information. It was estimated that Trump received over $1 billion of free publicity from networks taking his rallies and news conferences live.

Back to 2020, and with no way to hold live rallies due to the danger of the coronavirus, he would use official news conferences, such as the coronavirus task force news conferences, as campaign events. He would go off on tangents and make sure he was front and center of the news, even when his science experts were the people making the news by offering guidance and updates on the virus.

Tweets as news

At the beginning of the Trump presidency, there was a question as to whether tweets on Twitter should be considered official presidential communications, or if this was simply an outlet for the President to vent about his frustrations. After going back and forth on the matter, the Trump administration and the news informally decided that whatever the President tweets is an official communication. Subsequently, tweets have included official statements from the White House, but also rants about events or people he was battling against. The news started taking the President's tweets as official and would constantly criticize the President's tendency to re-tweet objectional content such as posts from white nationalists.

Rattling markets and minorities

The President, not having been a professional politician before holding office as President, had caused occasional havoc on stock markets when he would make pronouncements about relations with other countries (for example, with China), or with domestic corporations (anti-trust cases against Facebook and Google). The stock market would move up or down depending on his declarations of the day.

President Trump's base of voters in 2016 were working-class white men and women. In order to keep his voters happy and to consolidate his power, he seeded deep divisions amongst whites and blacks, especially in his handling of the Black Lives Matters movement after the killing of George Floyd. In fact, throughout his presidency, he baited his followers and the black community to create cultural friction.

Permission to be offensive & Emboldened Racists

After Trump's election in 2016, America saw an increase in hate crimes and a there was a sense that, at least among some, offensive speech had become acceptable. This was especially present at Trump rallies and campaign events, where attendees spoke openly about America being a "white country," and that others were not welcome. This gave rise to people like Richard Spencer, an open neo-Nazi and white supremacist, set out to regain America's "white identity." Although many say this type of hate speech did not re-emerge because of President Trump, Trump surely made hate speech more acceptable among his followers.

A Divided America

All of the things mentioned in this section about how the world has changed thanks to the election of President Trump in 2016, have lead to a divided America. It has lead to an America that inserted politics into everything, from who wore masks during the pandemic (Democrats were more likely to wear masks, while Republicans said masks restricted their freedoms), to which companies you bought your food from (Goya was famously boycotted by Latinos when its CEO went on television and made a statement in support of Trump).

All of these events have drastically changed the media landscape in America. Liberals have over-compensated in their quest for equity, and by doing so have helped eliminate problematic emblems of the past, such as Confederate statues, racist logos and names on food packaging, and have helped put measures into place to end the use of excessive force by police. Conservatives have also over-compensated in their quest to be lead by a "strong man," with Republican officials in every level of government acquiescing to Trump's demands in order to help their political careers in spite of the damage to the country.

ACTIVITY: Gender in the News

What you need: A copy of today's local newspaper or a print-out of a local news website and two markers of different colors.

How long it takes: The entire exercise including the discussion usually takes about an hour. The setup is usually about five minutes, the search is about 20 minutes, and the discussion is usually about 35 minutes.

What it teaches: Just because news outlets are "mass media", not everyone is equally represented in them.

Women have come a long way in regards to working in journalism and being represented in the media. The number of women working in news has grown exponentially since the 1940s.

But although the number of women working in the media has increased, has the ratio of women to men increased during that time? Or have both numbers increased in equal proportions?

To find out the answer, let us take a look at today's news.

The activity: Pick a section (front page, business, sports, etc.) and then find and circle the name of every woman you find. The name can be an article's author, a photographer, and even someone mentioned in a story. If the name is mentioned multiple times, only circle that name the first time you find it.

Now, take a different color pen or marker and circle the name of every man you find. Again, the name can be that of an author, a photographer, or someone mentioned in an article.

When you are done looking for all of the names, count up the names of all of the women you found, and do the same for all of the men you found. What is the percentage of men to women? Is it what you expected it to be? As a reference, doing this exercise on a newspaper from the late 1920s found about 8 times more men than women. Is today's newspaper different?

Try doing this exercise with different sections of the newspaper or news website. Do you find a different ratio of men to women in those different sections? Why do you think this discrepancy exists?

What is going on: Although we have come a long way in women's jobs since the 1940s, newspaper jobs and stories are still dominated by men? This is because the main audience for these newspapers is usually men, but more importantly, newspapers have not caught up with the rest of the media in terms of equal representation.

Newspaper sections also try to appeal to different people, so you may have noticed a more equal ratio in the Health section or the Food section. You may have also noticed almost no women mentioned in the sports section. To a large degree, these sections appeal to people based on stereotypes. These stereotypes say that most people who like sports are men, which is not as true as you would be lead to believe. The stereotypes also say that most people interested in health or food are women. The fact that these sections contain dieting tips and recipes helps reinforce these stereotypes.

What do the results from this exercise say about the media we consume? What does it say about our society? What would happen if news did not exist? Who benefits when news happens? Do those same people benefit when no news is happening? These are all questions we will attempt to answer as we do the following activities.

ACTIVITY: Minority News VS Majority News

What you need: A copy of today's local "mass market" newspaper (or a print-out of a local mainstream news website) and a copy of today's local "minority" newspaper for any minority group (or a print-out of a local minority news website).

How long it takes: The entire exercise including the discussion usually takes about an hour. The setup is usually about five minutes, the search is about 20 minutes, and the discussion is usually about 35 minutes.

What it teaches: Different groups of people will find different things important. Just because something is on the front page of the local "mass market" newspaper, that does not mean that a minority group will also feature the story on their front page.

Media are created with different people in mind. Each newspaper or news website, as well as any piece of media in general, aims to please a particular group of people. The more different a group is from another, the more their priorities will be different. A perfect example of this is a group in the "majority" and a group in the "minority".

The activity: Find a copy of today's local "mass market" newspaper, as well as a copy of a local minority newspaper (or websites, as previously mentioned). You may need to do some searching to find a copy of the minority newspaper. This is because, while mass market newspapers can be found easily on every corner, the minority newspapers will only be available in the areas where that minority group lives. These days you might find a copy of the local minority newspaper online, as well as on the news stand. The minority newspaper can belong to any minority, and can even be written in a language other than English. Try searching online for "<your city name> Spanish news" to get you started.

When you have either two newspapers or two web print-outs, compare them. First, take a look at the front pages of both newspapers. Are there similar stories on both front pages? Remember that each group might prioritize certain stories over others, so you might not see the same headlines on both papers. What do the front page stories tell you about what is important to the group of people that the newspaper appeals to? Are there any similarities?

When you are done with the front page, go on to both newspapers' other sections. Are the front page stories the same in each newspaper? You may find that the sections are in different order, for example, in one newspaper the sports section might follow the front page and in another the business section might follow it. You might also find that the newspapers do not have the same sections, for example, one newspaper might not have a home and garden section or a business section. What do these things tell you about what the newspapers' audiences find important?

After you are done looking at the stories in the different sections, start looking at the advertisements in each paper. What kind of ads appear in the mass market newspaper compared to the minority newspaper? Are they similar or different? If an advertiser has placed an ad in both newspapers, how are the two ads different? What types of products and services are advertised in each newspaper? This might tell you a lot about what the newspaper's audience is like.

What is going on: Since the newspapers appeal to different groups of people, they are likely to have different top stories in each section. When the stories are similar, you are likely to find a different perspective in the two stories. For example, each newspaper tries to answer the question "why do my readers care about this?" when they pick their stories. The reporters and editors will tailor the newspaper to the readers' interests.

The advertisements in the newspaper also tell you a lot about what the audience wants to buy, or can afford to buy. If the advertisements are for expensive luxury items, the newspaper as a whole probably appeals to wealthier people. But if the newspaper contains ads for discount stores, this tells you that the majority of its readers likely cannot afford luxury goods. You can get a pretty good idea about who the reader is by looking at the ads and the stories. You can probably tell what the average income is among readers, as well as their political views.

ACTIVITY: The People Giving Us the News

What you need: A television tuned to an evening newscast on a local station. If this is for a class, this can be done as homework, or it can be done in class by using a recording of last night's local newscast.

How long it takes: The entire exercise including the discussion (or written analysis for homework) usually takes about two hours. The viewing takes 30 minutes to an hour, and the discussion (or analysis) is usually about 30 minutes to an hour.

What it teaches: We learn about the world from these people on TV, but who are they? We learn that the people bringing us the news are not necessarily like us, but they are entertaining and supposedly "credible", even though they are essentially just actors reading a script.

The activity: The first part of this activity is to watch an evening newscast on a local television station. We want to make sure that we watch the news on a local station and not a 24-hour news network, since the way each organization presents the news is quite different. With a local newscast, we get a tight one-hour broadcast with the day's events instead of on-going news from a 24-hour news channel.

Take a close examination of the news anchors in the studio and the reporters out in the field. What do these people look like? Are there more women or men as anchors and reporters? Do the men act differently than the women? Do the women look the way women look in other media (like models or actresses)?

What ethnicity are the people who bring us the news? Are they the same ethnicity as you? Do you think it makes a difference if the anchors and reporters are the same ethnicity as you or not? How would you view the anchors differently if they were originally from a country you've never heard of and they speak with an accent?

How old are the anchors and reporters that bring us the news? Are they teenagers, in their 20s and 30s, middle-aged, or practically senior citizens? Are the women, on average, older or younger than the men? Why do you think that is?

What makes these anchors and reporters qualified to tell us the news? Do they hold advanced degrees in journalism, or are they just actors playing a role? Do they sound like they have experience discussing the topics they are talking about? Is there a difference in the appearance of the people who tell us the main stories and those who tell us about the weather, sports, and entertainment? What are those differences?

What is going on: The people who bring us the news have a great responsibility to their audience. We learn about our world through their eyes. But the people who bring us the news are not always as qualified to do so as you may think. Some do not have degrees, and many who have degrees do not have degrees in journalism. In fact, most anchors do not even write the stories themselves, so the news comes from faceless writers who may look nothing like these people.

We also pay important attention to certain appearances. When we get the news, we want credible information. The people bringing us the news know that credible appearances matter so many male anchors are old and gray, giving them a credible appearance. And many female news anchors actually look like men as well – short hair, wearing a suit, subtle makeup, and speaking with a deeper voice. You will also notice that most male anchors are older than their female counterparts.

The anchors and reporters also tend to look and sound like their audience – a mainly white viewing audience will likely have more white reporters. This is the same reason Spanish broadcasts do not employ non-native Spanish speakers – it is about connecting with the audience and giving the appearance of credibility.

ACTIVITY: The Lead Story

What you need: A television tuned to an evening newscast on a local station. If this is for a class, this can be done as homework, or it can be done in class by using a recording of last night's local newscast.

How long it takes: The entire exercise including the discussion (or written analysis for homework) usually takes about an hour. The viewing takes 10-20 minutes, and the discussion (or analysis) is usually about 30-40 minutes.

What it teaches: The news media have teams of people trying to decide what stories to run in the evening newscast. They select these stories based on who the intended audience is. This means that the lead story is not meant to be "the biggest story in the world", but instead "the biggest story to the viewer".

The activity: Watch an evening newscast on either a local television station, or on a 24-hour news network. This activity works best if you start watching from the beginning of the newscast or at the top of each hour.

When you watch, ask yourself who the newscast's intended audience is. Is it mostly men or women?

Would kids be interested in the newscast? Would seniors be interested in the stories presented? How can you tell who the audience is for the newscast? Do the advertisements give us any clue?

Every newscast begins with the "top story" as their very first story, and someone has to decide what that story will be. What is the lead story in this newscast? Why did the people in charge decide this story would be the lead story and not the second or third story? Is the story important to society as a whole, or just to the local area and just to a particular group of people? Is the lead story positive or negative in nature?

Does this story affect the intended audience? How? Why did the people in charge believe the lead story would matter to the audience? Is this story interesting to you? Why or why not? Watching the newscast's first segment (the stories before the first commercial), would you have chosen a different top story if you were in charge? What story would you have chosen and why?

What is going on: Newscasts always lead with the most sensational or impactful story that it is audience would find interesting. Chances are that your local evening newscast began with a local shooting or murder of some sort – this is typically as sensational and impactful as stories get. There is an old saying in local news – “If it bleeds, it leads.” This story placement is meant to get the audience drawn into the newscast and have them stay tuned for later stories. This means that the bigger the lead story, the better it is for the newscast.

The intended audiences for these evening newscasts are usually middle-aged and older people. This is proven when you hear the news anchors say things like “how this (or that) might affect your kids”, and also by the ads that try to sell things to people with families, houses, and cars. Even though anyone can watch the newscast – evening newscasts are usually not titled “Local Newscast for African Americans aged 30-55” – the newscast does try to appeal to a specific audience and not everyone in general. Keep this in mind the next time you watch a newscast. Ask yourself if the newscast was created with your interests in mind, or if they are trying to appeal to someone else.

Why do newscasts try so hard to appeal to their audience? The reason is because the more appealing the news stories and reporting style, the more people will watch. When more people watch, the television station can ask advertisers for more money to place an ad during that newscast. So essentially, a more appealing newscast means more money in the station's pockets.

Alternate activity: You can also try this activity by using a newspaper instead of a newscast. Instead of the lead story, look at the top headline or photograph on the front page. Why did the newspaper editor believe that this story would appeal most to the newspaper's audience? Newspapers use headlines and photos on their front page to entice people to buy the issue from the newsstand. The more impactful the headline or photo, the more newspapers they will sell.

What you need: A television tuned to an evening newscast on a local station. If this is for a class, this can be done as homework, or it can be done in class by using a recording of last night's local newscast.

How long it takes: The entire exercise including the discussion (or written analysis for homework) usually takes about an hour. The viewing takes about an hour, and the discussion (or analysis) is usually also about an hour.

What it teaches: There are a lot of things that go into the creation of a newscast. News editors must come up with the story assignments for the day. Reporters must gather stories and interview people, camera people must video tape the scene, and video editors must edit together the footage and add graphics and music. These elements are all a part of the process of bringing us the information we receive.

The activity: Watch an evening newscast on either a local television station, or on a 24-hour news network. This activity works best if you start watching from the beginning of the newscast or at the top of each hour.

Keep track of the newscast's stories by writing them down in a numbered list as they play. Try categorizing the stories by indicating their geographical appeal – local, national, or international. Also keep track of whether each story is a positive story (like a dog rescue or feeding the homeless) or a negative story (like death and destruction of property).

When the newscast ends, go back and tally the totals for the geographic appeal and for the positive-to-negative story ratio. Are the stories mostly local appeal, national appeal, or international appeal? Did you feel that more importance was placed on one type or another? Did you like this balance? Are the stories mostly positive or negative? If an alien was watching this newscast, would it think this was a bad world or a good world? From your own experience, would you agree with the alien's conclusion? Do you think the newscast fairly balances the portrayal of good and bad things in the world, or does it focus too much on one or the other?

What is going on: The news does not just happen. Events happen every minute of every day all around the world. The job of the news reporting industry is to pick the stories they believe their audience would be most interested in and show them only those stories. Any story that does not meet these criteria is not included in the newscast.

We experience the world in a very linear way – we see things happen in real time and in chronological order. The news media are not restricted by our own limitations. They can edit out parts of reality that are less important, include only the parts they feel add positively to the events, and they can rearrange the events so that they tell a story. An event that occurred over a five hour period can be summed up in a 20-second story using clever narration and video editing.

There is also a very definite language and process used by news reporters to bring us the news. This formula ensures that the news is not only informative, but that it is also entertaining. After all, what happens to the news if no one is interested in watching it? The newscasters look and sound like their audience. The editors pick stories that evoke emotions in us – happiness, anger, fear, etc.

News producers use various techniques to keep us interested. Instead of just aiming a camera at an event, they have an excited reporter speaking on camera. Newscasts usually always have interesting tugs that help evoke emotions, and interesting graphics that fly across the screen to capture our attention.

ACTIVITY: 24-Hour News Networks

What you need: A television tuned to a 24-hour cable news network. The newscast can be watched live or pre-recorded and viewed later on video.

How long it takes: The entire exercise including the discussion (or written analysis for homework) usually takes about an hour. The viewing takes about an hour, and the discussion (or analysis) is usually also about an hour.

What it teaches: 24-hour news networks must run news, as their names suggest, for 24 hours each day. This means that they need material to fill those 24 hours. That means that they may end up airing un-news (stories that are of no real consequence) just to fill time. Since they do not tell us "this is just filler", even these small stories influence us and inform our worldview.

The activity: Watch an evening newscast on either a 24-hour news network. This activity works best if you start watching from the beginning of the newscast or at the top of each hour.

Take note of the stories being shown. How many stories are shown in a single hour? If there are only a few stories (5 or less), do they all seem important? If there are many stories (10 or more), do these stories seem less important? Are there any important stories or topics that are news in your mind but they are not showing for some reason?

Take a look at the production techniques for the newscast. Is the "most important" story being aired with dramatic graphics and music, or on its own with only location images and sound? How do each of these techniques affect how you interpret the stories?

What is going on: 24-hour news networks must fill 24 hours per day with news. But what happens when nothing "important" (to the network's audience) is going on in the world? In this case they need to fill the airwaves with smaller stories from around the country or the world. These stories are usually not as dramatic as "big" stories, but instead are usually fun or "human interest" stories (like a pet that saved his owner, for example).

When a huge story hits the news wires (a bombing or a shooting), the networks focus their attention on just this story. What ends up happening is that when a lot of news is going on (the big stories), there are less stories on the news network since they are focusing on just this one big story. When there is nothing happening, there are a lot of smaller stories airing for shorter amounts of time each. And when absolutely no news is happening (a "slow news day"), the top story might be something as minor as "squirrel steals schoolgirl's lunch".

The most interesting part of 24-hour news networks is that they get the most viewers when something really bad happens in the world. As soon as something bad happens, many people turn to these news networks to get the latest information and video from the events. Remember that 24-hour news networks are businesses out to make money. The more viewers they get, the more money they make from advertising. And the more bad things happen, the more viewers they get. In other words, peace on earth would mean an end for these networks.

Today, 24-hour news networks are taking a cue from the internet by allowing viewers to add their own videos and comments directly from their cell phones. This has obvious benefits – this means that a) they can spend less money trying to "break" a hot story, b) they get more content to help fill those 24-hours, and c) they get viewers involved, which helps keep other viewers engaged and tuned in.

ACTIVITY: Current Events

What you need: A copy of today's newspaper or a news website. The news outlet could be local or national, but it should be a "mainstream" news outlet, and not a small community news outlet. Examples of mainstream news outlet are HuffPost.com or CNN.com, while small community examples are SMMirror.com or LaOpinion.com.

How long it takes: The initial setup can take anywhere from 5 minutes to 20 minutes. The newspaper review portion can also take 5 to 20 minutes. The discussion portion can be as short as 5 minutes, and as long as desired.

What it teaches: What we typically think are important current events happening around us are not always the same things that newspapers believe are important. There is often a disconnect between what we believe is an important issue that should be covered in the news, and what the people in the news industry believe should be covered. There is an especially large disconnect when those who are not members of a newspaper's typical audience are asked to determine what news stories are important.

The activity: Think about some hot news stories happening right now. The stories could be of local importance, or they could be of national or international significance. If your group chose to focus on a specific part of society, such as business or sports current events, use only those sections of the paper for this activity. The stories could be very current, such as the results of a sporting event, or they could be general events happening on an ongoing basis, such as an ongoing social crisis.

After you have gathered about 10-12 responses, take a look at the front page of your chosen newspaper or section of the newspaper. Are the stories your group mentioned the same as the stories on the front page of the paper? If not, why is there a disconnect between their opinion of what is important, and the newspaper's opinion of what to print and make important? If people guessed some of the stories correctly, what does that say about them as members of the newspaper's audience? Who determines what the top stories are? Do the top stories just appear and ask to be printed, or is someone choosing these stories? Are there any stories that just do not make any sense as front page items? Why does the group think each story was chosen to be on the front page, and not on one of the inside pages? Why are some of the stories the group chose not on the front page?

What is going on: Just like all media, newspapers aim their content at specific people (target market). Usually, the target market for newspapers is older people, many with at least some higher education and with higher than average incomes. You could always determine a newspaper's target market by looking at the products being sold in the ads. This means that, although a newspaper is called the "(local city) Times" or "(local city) Herald", the newspaper does not aim towards every single person in that city, but only a small portion of it.

If your group is not a part of the news outlet's target audience, then their opinions on what are important stories may be different than the opinions of someone who is a part of the paper's target audience. While younger people may be more interested in social issues and news about topics interesting to them, many older readers are interested in different topics that may be affecting them. For example, while younger people may be interested in youth culture, war, and style, older readers may be more interested in news about taxes, child care, and employment. Although there may be people in both groups interested in things that are of interest to the other group, newspapers know what most of their readers want and they try their best to give it to them – it helps them sell papers.

In addition, the newspaper does not always keep the most important stories in the headlines. In order to keep readers interested, newspaper editors need to refresh their top stories every day or so, meaning that stories that are still important may be sent to a space on the inside. Newspapers need to be as current as possible, and attract its target market as much as possible, and so the stories you believe should be top stories are not always the kind of attention-getters the newspapers are looking for.

Chapter 8 – Video Games

Video games have gained in popularity since their introduction in the late 1970s. Today, the video game industry is a multi-billion dollar annual industry, with hundreds of new titles released every year. One of the main reasons for the expansion in this industry is the broadening of video games' appeal from the typical male teen playing a game on his console at home, to games that appeal to just about everyone and are available on a variety of devices. In fact, the largest growth area in the video games industry is in the area of casual games, games that can be played for free on social media sites like Facebook or on smartphones and tablets. Games are now being played, not just by those teenage boys in their bedrooms, but by toddlers, seniors and retirees, stay-at-home mothers and fathers, corporate executives, college students, and everyone in between.

Video games have also become more addictive than ever. Most studies show that the average time we play video games has gone up over the years. Game makers have found new ways to keep us hooked on games, including connecting them to social media so we can compete against friends. Some popular games are Angry Birds, Words With Friends, and Candy Crush Saga (played on smartphones and tablets), the Grand Theft Auto series and Electronic Arts' sports series (played on home gaming consoles), and that is just to name a few.

Since video games are so popular, and we spend so much time with them, they are worth exploring further. Video games are similar to movies, television shows, and literature in that they usually tell a story with characters and situations, but they are different because the player is the main character in the story, and they get to determine how the story ends (or at least many of the events along the way). Video games often stand in for a substitute for real life, allowing us to experience a different world or environment without leaving the safety of our homes. Just as with others types of media, video games have the capability to influence behavior and psychology, which is then exhibited in real life. Let us explore video games a bit further and learn how they influence us, and how we can make sense of these influences.

What are games?

We can describe a game as a formal way to play – so it's play (like we did as children), but with formal boundaries – rules, challenges, ways to interact with an opponent, etc. This is different than just playing by running around and yelling, which is what many young children do when they begin to play. By adding formal rules, challenges, and ways to interact with an opponent, you turn running and yelling into a game like Hide and Seek.

The way humans play games has evolved over thousands of years. Typically, games require two or more people to participate, and it has only been in the past 50 years or so that computers have made it possible to play "against the computer" or to play one-player games. As games evolved from activities of community and culture to activities of distraction and "killing time," the types of games we play have changed as well. While video games used to be marketed to teenage boys, today's smartphone-laden world has made games go mainstream, with thousands of developers creating games for just about anyone. Today's video game industry is the largest of any other media industry, earning more annual revenue than the movie and television industries.

Elements of Games

What types of elements make up the games in different game categories? Would you know how to tell the difference between a shooter game compared to an RPG? Similar to movies and television, games can be categorized into groupings called genres. The following is a list of popular video game genres and some representative games in each.

- **Action** (Street Fighter, Counter Strike, Halo)
- **Adventure** (Resident Evil, Tomb Raider)
- **Simulation** (build, emulate reality – The Sims, Flight Sim)
- **RPG** (usually fantasy, emulates board games – WOW, Final Fantasy)
- **Puzzles** (Tetris, Candy Crush)
- **Sports** (Madden NFL, NBA Live)
- **Music** (Guitar Hero)
- **Non-traditional** (Wii Fit, Wii Sports)
- **Casual** (Farmville, Angry Birds, Cut The Rope)
- **Word** (Words with Friends)

These are just some of the genres and games popular today. The audiences taste in genres evolves continually, so a type of game that is popular today may not be popular in a year. Just like with other media, video games segment their audiences based on characteristics like age, gender, and interests. A game's target audience can be determined by the game's genre, the platform (smartphone or console?), and the characteristics of how the game functions. Here are some things to consider when you try to better understand a game, its audience, and how it works.

- **Game mechanics** – how does the game work? Do you slide pieces of candy in different directions to try to clear the board? Are you driving a car and trying to reach a goal before the time runs out?
- **Audio** – what does the game sound like? Are the sound effects realistic, or are they synthesized sounds? A flight simulator is likely to have realistic sounds while a game like Mario Kart will have imaginary sounds that are meant to be amusing.

- **Visuals** – what does the game look like? Does the art tell you that the game takes place in the real world, or is this an imaginary world?
- **Programming** – how does the game operate? Do you use your finger, a dedicated controller, or some other means to complete the game objective? What elements of the game tell you if you have succeeded or failed? Can you play with friends, or is it a single player game?
- **Game activities** – What kinds of things do you do in the game? Some common game activities are racing, shooting, commanding, hiding, trading, escaping, finding, solving puzzles. Some activities are exclusive to certain genres, but many games may allow the player to perform several of these activities.
- **Story** – what is the game about? Most games have a story or at minimum they try to tell you something about the world in which it takes place. Some games may have elaborate stories written by experienced storytellers, while others may just tell you that you have some empty land and it is up to you to create your own story.

There is a lot to know about games to help you better understand how they work. Like with all media, the best way to understand games is to play them. If there is a game you have heard good or bad things about, try playing it and see if you can understand the game from a media literacy perspective. The following activities will help you better understand video games.

Appendix: Video Game-related Learning Activities

ACTIVITY: Violence in Video Games

What you need: A video game on any platform, whether it be on a console connected to a television, a game on the internet or on a computer, or a game on a tablet or smartphone, in which the player plays as a main character.

How long it takes: Approximately 30 minutes.

What it teaches: This exercise teaches how to recognize violence in video games, including in games that do not seem so violent.

The activity: Play some of the chosen video game, or watch some video of the gameplay from that game. Does the game seem violent to you? Why or why not? What type of violence is happening on screen, if any? If you think that the game seems violent, what level of violence does the game display, on a scale of 1 to 10? Why do you think the game developer decided to include or not include violence in the game? Does the game's target market find violence appealing? What would parents say about the violence in the game? Do you think a violent game would sell more copies than a non-violent game? Why or why not?

What is going on: Most games that feature a main character of some sort include some level of violence. Violence does not have to involve shooting or stabbing or running people over with a car. Violence can be as subtle as the main character running through a maze while knocking over anything (or anybody) in its way. All levels of violence can be influential in some way to the game's player. This is especially true when the game fails to show any consequences for being violent. In fact, quite the opposite is often true; the main character in the game is both the aggressor and the hero.

ACTIVITY: Fantasy in Video Games

What you need: A video game on any platform, whether it be on a console connected to a television, a game on the internet or on a computer, or a game on a tablet or smartphone.

How long it takes: Approximately 30 minutes.

What it teaches: This activity teaches that video games take place in a fantasy world, and that the stories, characters, actions, tasks, situations, and environment rarely take place in real life.

The activity: Play the video game or show a video of the game being played for approximately five minutes. Then consider the elements in the video game that reflect (or do not reflect) things that exist in real life. Some things to consider are, does the character have any super powers, can the character "die" and come back to life to play the level again, does time move more slowly or more quickly than in real life, do the characters in the game exist in real life, and would this situation ever really happen in real life? Compare the events and situations happening in the game with your own life. Is your life ever this exciting? How would you feel if you were the character in real life? How does playing this game make you feel? Why do people find the game appealing to play?

What is going on: Games take place in fantasy worlds that usually do not reflect real life. Game makers try to create experiences that allow players to experience a fantasy, all without the need to be in any danger. Players can feel what it might be like to battle dragons in medieval times, all without leaving the comfort of their chair. This acts as a distraction and entertainment for players looking to escape reality for a while. Game makers try to fulfill the player's fantasy by giving them experiences that do not happen in real life. For example, no one would likely play a game in which they need to clean the house, finish their homework, and brush their teeth; this is real life, and it is usually boring.

ACTIVITY: Ads in Video Games

What you need: A free, ad-supported video game on any platform, whether it be on a console connected to a television, a game on the internet or on a computer, or a game on a tablet or smartphone.

How long it takes: Approximately 30 minutes.

What it teaches: Today's video games often have advertising in them, either directly (as with banner ads in an online or mobile game), or indirectly (as with games with brand placements). This activity will teach how to analyze a game with an advertisement, and how to tell that something is being sold to the player.

The activity: Play the video game or show a video of the game being played for approximately five minutes. Keep track of any advertisements in the game, either in the form of a banner ad (usually at the bottom or between levels on a mobile game, or sometimes on the edges of the screen for an online game), or in the form of brand placement (in which a product is actually a part of the game, like a logo on a character's shirt or a car the character drives).

If this game appeals to you, think about why a particular advertisement or product was shown to you. Why does the game's maker think you would want to see that advertisement in the game? Do you think the ad is interrupting the way you play the game? Why or why not does the ad seem intrusive? Would you ever buy a product featured in or advertised in a game? Why or why not?

What is going on: Just like with television and radio, video games use advertisements to earn extra revenue, maybe in addition to charging a fee for the game or maybe instead of charging a fee, as is the case with many mobile games. The game maker typically has an idea of who is playing their game, and they attract advertisers to pay money to be seen in the game by those players. To the game maker, including advertising means they make more money than just charging the one-time fee for the game, which often means they can give away the game for free and only make money with the ads. This is a benefit to players because they do not have to pay for the game. It is also a benefit to the game maker because a free game will typically have more people playing it than a paid game. And it is a benefit to the advertiser because they get to show their ad to the player.

ACTIVITY: Characters in Video Games

What you need: A video game on any platform, whether it be on a console connected to a television, a game on the internet or on a computer, or a game on a tablet or smartphone.

How long it takes: Approximately 30 minutes.

What it teaches: This activity teaches how to recognize the characters and character types that exist in video games.

The activity: Play the video game or show a video of the game being played for approximately five minutes. This should be sufficient time to learn about the characters, the game's situation or story, and the world that the game takes place in.

Then, make a list of the main characters in the game and identify them with a single adjective. For example, the main character (probably the player's character) is likely the hero. There is also probably one or several villains, along with several other "bad guys" and "good guys". After the list is made, attempt to analyze how each character is portrayed. Ask yourself, why is the hero the good guy and why is the villain the bad guy? What kind of stereotypes are used for each character? What real life characteristics does each character embody? Do you agree or disagree with how each character is portrayed?

What is going on: The characters in video games are supposed to be easy to understand, often at first glance. This means that the characters typically exhibit stereotypical features that make them easy to understand. But we know that in real life, people are complex and often are not easy to characterize. Often, the hero in video games is the aggressor and the villain might be the victim. Video games try to keep things simple for players, but that oversimplification often distorts reality and makes things that are typically perceived as wrong seem alright.

Chapter 9 – Radio and Other Audio-Based Media

Radio has been around since the early part of the 20th century. It was the first type of electronic media that allowed people to get live entertainment in their homes. At the time, radio competed with other media like newspapers, movies, and theatre.

Today, radio faces strong competition from other types of media vying for people's attention. Besides competing with television and movies, radio has had to compete with personal music devices like iPods, as well as with local radio alternatives like satellite radio.

Radio is unique in that it provides live information and entertainment without the use of any visuals. In fact, the only things that radio uses to get its messages across are voices, music, and sound effects; the listener is in charge of providing perspective and for internalizing radio's messages.

Despite what sounds like a limiting factor (only using sound to get the message across), those sounds carry their weight in getting the message across. Just imagine how much you are affected by a piece of music you hear on the radio. A song can put you in a mood, and radio advertisers know this. The same goes for the types of voices used in radio. A voice can have many qualities to it – tone, depth, loudness, accent, and tempo – all aspects of a voice that can make you feel a certain way. A loud sound effect can shift your attention from your driving to the message coming in over the radio. With just these three sound elements, radio has the power to create a compelling message with embedded values and ideas.

A current form of radio – which is not delivered over the airwaves at all but instead is delivered over the internet – is podcasting. Podcasting first gained popularity in the mid-2000s thanks to the advent of inexpensive audio recording equipment that allowed anyone to create a podcast show from their homes with little money. As podcasting matured, it became more of a medium to hear your favorite shows from NPR and other professional radio producers, and less of a medium that democratized the creation and distribution of ideas. While small-time podcasters have struggled to find success in recent years, its popularity due to shows like *This American Life* and *Serial* cannot be denied.

From a media literacy perspective, we want to pay attention to the messages we hear on the radio and in podcasts, and not let them just pass our ears without a second thought. Even if you say you do not listen to radio or podcasts that often, if you are out in public at all or you listen to music, you are exposed to the effects of radio.

The Elements of Radio and Podcasts

To better understand how radio and podcasts affect us, it is useful to understand the components, or elements, of this medium. There are four main components of radio and podcasting: voice, music, sound effects, and writing. Let us explore each one.

Voice

The voice's role in audio media is to deliver the explicit message in the script. This means that the voice tells us precisely what the writer wants us to know about the subject. In a radio commercial, the voice tells us about the product, why we should buy it, and where to buy it. In a podcast or radio show, the voice belongs to a host who might share a story or some information with us.

While the voice's primary objective is to directly convey a message, there are many creative techniques used to help make the message more interesting. For example, a commercial might have an announcer telling us about a product, but it may also contain a story with two characters interacting with the product somehow. The story or vignette helps the keep the audience interested and also helps the audience associate with the product. So if you are listening to a fast food commercial, it might feature two college students discussing dinner options. If you are a college student, you will relate to this dialogue and perhaps imagine yourself in this very situation. The advertiser hopes that you have had the same problem as the characters and that their solution to the problem will be your solution as well.

The voice in audio media can also help create meaning in a particular message. Casting directors hire voice actors who will support the overall message, often by using stereotypes to quickly give meaning to a script. For example, what are the characteristics that you associate with a British accent? I will bet that you likely think “sophisticated,” “refined,” and “classy.” Producers and casting directors know this, so they hire voice actors with British accents when they want to associate those characteristics with their products.

Music

The music in an audio production is chosen for its ability to contribute to and support the overall message. Just like selecting the right voice is important, selecting the right piece of music is also very important. As an example, think about the emotions that you associate with upbeat classical music. You might think “happy” or “excited” when you hear this type of music. If the purpose of a particular commercial is to get the listener excited, the producer will pick a piece of music that best invokes that particular emotion in the listener. An example of this might be a commercial for a theme park – the music, combined with an excited announcer, can help make the theme park sound exciting without using any visuals.

Sound Effects

Sound effects help further the effect of reality for the listener, and helps paint a picture of the scene without using any visuals. Imagine for example that you are listening to a commercial about an auto repair shop. The commercial might start with the sound effect of a car screeching and then crashing. This serves two purposes. Since the sound effect occurs at the beginning, it is an attention getter, making you instantly shift your attention to the commercial if you were doing something else. It also helps tell the listener what is happening. Most of us have heard and maybe even seen a car crash, so we can imagine what it looks like just by listening to the sound of it.

Writing

The writing in audio media is what brings together all of the other elements to create a cohesive message. The writing's tone will help convey a particular message and make the listener feel a particular way. For example, imagine a public service announcement (a PSA is a kind of a commercial that is meant to raise awareness about an issue) about heart disease. The PSA's purpose is to inform the public about the dangers of obesity and the benefits of exercise. What kind of tone is appropriate for this type of message? Should it be funny, sad, urgent, scary, or happy? How should the announcer read the script – fast, slow, with a smile on their face? What type of music should be in the background to help reinforce the message? Should the PSA have any sound effects like a heart beating or a beeping heart monitor? All of these decisions are made in the writing phase of the project, and everything must come together to create a cohesive whole.

Here is a sample 15-second PSA script about heart disease.

Heart Disease PSA - :15

MUSIC: Slow drone
SFX: Heart beating, beeping heart monitor

ANNOUNCER (somber): Someone dies from heart disease every 90 seconds in the US.

MUSIC STOPS
SFX: Heart beat stops, heart monitor flat lines

ANNOUNCER: Don't be a statistic. Follow a healthy diet and find time to exercise. Learn more at heart dot org.

The script has everything the producer needs to know about how the commercial should sound to convey the appropriate message. All of the elements work together to create a cohesive message.

Now that we have explored how sound can be used without visuals to convey a powerful message, let us dig deeper with the following activities.

ACTIVITY: Voices in Commercials

What you need: A variety of radio commercials, either taped from the airwaves, or downloaded from the websites of various companies who produce radio commercials.

How long it takes: Each commercial lasts either 30 or 60 seconds, and can be analyzed in about 5 minutes. Analyze as many or as few commercials as time permits.

What it teaches: Radio producers only have three elements to capture our attention: voice, music, and sound effects. They use these elements to make their audience have an emotional response to what is being advertised. As a society, we feel certain emotions when we hear certain voices. Radio casting directors play off of our emotional responses by casting actors – deejays – who can play characters we can relate to: the upper class gentleman, the "regular guy", the "ditzy girl" – all can be played by capable actors.

The activity: Listen to some radio advertisements. Specifically focus on the voices you hear in the commercial, and the emotions they make you feel. How does the voice affect how you hear the ad? Does the voice itself capture your attention, either because it has an accent or because the actor is playing a recognizable character? Or does the character say things that will make us want to listen to the commercial, such as something relatable to the commercial's target audience? Is the voice deep or high-pitched, and how does this affect your opinion about the character and the product? Does the character have an accent, and if so, what kind? Why do you think the casting director hired the actors that she did? What emotions do the characters make you feel? Excitement? Anxiety? Happiness? How do the characters' voices help sell the product or service being advertised?

What is going on: Advertisers are doing their jobs if they can somehow make us relate to the product or service being sold. They try to make us feel happy, sad, excited, liked, safe, weak, and powerful. They do this by using a combination of voice, music, and sound effects, playing off of our recognition of stereotypes. Advertisers only have 30 or 60 seconds to get our attention and get us interested in a product, so stereotypes are an easy answer to a question.

For example, if you were selling a high-end product to affluent customers (or people who would like to appear affluent), what voice might you cast to play the role of someone wealthy, dignified, and sophisticated? If we only had a few seconds to tell the audience that this character has all of those characteristics, a well-known stereotype might be the easy answer. Perhaps the casting director could cast a well-spoken actor with a British accent. This is because, in our society, a British accent is said to mean wealthy, dignified, and sophisticated. On the other hand, if you are selling a product to young beach goers, you might use the "surfer dude" stereotype as the character to sell your product. However, you would never hire a surfer dude to be the announcer for your wealth management banking service, unless you want your customers to think twice about using your service.

Stereotypes are usually used negatively in the media, but they can also be used positively. Regardless of how they are used, stereotypes are an important tool in the media creator's bag of tricks. Stereotypes are easy answers to difficult questions. Radio commercials need to tell you all they can about a particular character without the benefit of showing him or her to the audience. Using a character with stereotypical vocal attributes quickly answers the question "who is this character?" Learning to recognize this trick is an important part of understanding the influence of radio commercials.

ACTIVITY: Music in Commercials

What you need: A variety of radio commercials, either recorded from the airwaves, or downloaded from the websites of various companies who produce radio commercials.

How long it takes: Each commercial lasts either 30 or 60 seconds, and can be analyzed in about 5 minutes. Analyze as many or as few commercials as time permits.

What it teaches: Radio producers only have three elements to capture our attention: voice, music, and sound effects. They use these elements to make their audience have an emotional response to what is being advertised. As a society, we feel certain emotions when we hear certain pieces of music. Radio producers play off of our emotional responses by using the music that most resonates with us in that situation.

The activity: Listen to some radio advertisements. Specifically focus on the music you hear in the commercial. How does the music contribute to the commercial? How would you describe the music being used? Upbeat? Inspirational? Does the music fit with the situation or product being sold? Does the music give you a positive feeling? Why do you think the producer chose that music? How do the characters fit in with the music? Who is the commercial's intended audience? Do you think the music appeals to the intended audience?

What is going on: As a society, we have been raised to have emotional responses to particular types of music. After watching thousands of movies and TV shows, we have been conditioned to think or feel something for each piece of music we hear. In fact, we can often attribute a piece of music to a particular emotion. For example, when we hear classical music containing notes played in a major chord, high pitched wind and string instruments and played at a moderate tempo, we might feel excited or upbeat. And when we hear music played at a slow tempo with deep, minor chords, we might feel sad or melancholic.

Music does not just control our emotions – it helps to make us think about specific ideas. As a society, we have been conditioned to think of a detuned, twangy guitar as a sign we are in the old west. Or we might know that a scene takes place in Hawaii when we hear the traditional Ukuleles playing in the background. In movies, we often hear French horns played in big action sequences, and so we associated French horns with cinematic grandeur. These are only a few examples of how music can focus our emotions or train of thought.

Typically, radio producers want to use music as a major tool in the toolbox, since listeners do not have visuals to put them at a location. Music also sets the tone for the commercial – whether it is funny, sad, heroic, or jazzy, radio producers can find a piece of music to fit perfectly with the scenes. Often, the music reinforces the voice and sound effects, helping the listeners paint a complete picture in their minds. As an audience, we recognize when the music meets our expectations for a particular scene or story. In fact, inappropriate music often sticks out like a sore thumb. For example, imagine if a radio producer chose to use surfer music in a bank commercial that also used a British announcer. Unless the commercial intended to use humor in the ad, listeners are likely to find the music inappropriate.

ACTIVITY: The Writing in Commercials

What you need: A variety of radio commercials, either recorded from the airwaves, or downloaded from the websites of various companies who produce radio commercials.

How long it takes: Each commercial lasts either 30 or 60 seconds, and can be analyzed in about 5 minutes. Analyze as many or as few commercials as time permits.

What it teaches: Radio producers only have three elements to capture our attention: voice, music, and sound effects. But the writing in radio commercials is what brings all of these elements together. Radio writers use a variety of techniques to get our attention and make us interested in what is being said (and sold). By being able to recognize these techniques, we can be savvier radio listeners and avoid being persuaded without our knowledge.

The activity: Listen to some radio advertisements. Specifically focus on the way the commercial was written. How does the writer grab your attention? Does the commercial use drama or comedy to attract your attention? Can you imagine the world the commercial has created through sound effects, the writing, and the overall tone? Does the commercial make you want to buy the product? Why or why not? Are you the commercial's intended audience? How can you tell?

What is going on: Like all types of media, radio uses a unique language to disseminate its message and influence society. Radio lacks the visual elements taken for granted in media like television and the internet. So instead of visuals, radio focuses instead on providing an enjoyable listening experience. Radio producers use voice, music, and sound effects to tell stories and help their listeners' minds imagine the world. But none of this could be possible without the writing that must take place before anything is ever recorded or edited. Radio writers understand the need to show the world through sound, and they use various techniques to get people's attention.

Often times, the script can be as simple as calling for a particular type of voice actor to play a role. When writing characters, radio writers want to be sure they make the character relatable to the audience. In fact, frequently the main character in a radio commercial is identical in demographic as the commercial's audience. Writing relatable characters is only one way radio commercial writers get our attention.

Humor is very prominent in radio, especially radio commercials. Not only does this help give the commercial an opportunity to stand out from other programming, but it also helps get and keep the audience's attention. Humor is one of the only dramatic elements that translates well whether an image exists or not. This is one of the reasons many old-time radio shows used humor instead of drama or horror to frame their stories.

Learning to recognize styles of writing in radio will help audiences better understand the techniques that radio producers use to reach their audiences.

ACTIVITY: What Is Being Sold?

What you need: A variety of radio commercials, either recorded from the airwaves, or downloaded from the websites of various companies who produce radio commercials.

How long it takes: Each commercial lasts either 30 or 60 seconds, and can be analyzed in about 5 minutes. Analyze as many or as few commercials as time permits.

What it teaches: Radio commercials, just like most advertisements, do not sell the product itself. Instead, they focus on selling a particular lifestyle or image to the audience. Learning about the ways that media influences us to buy is an important part of media literacy.

The activity: Listen to some radio advertisements. Specifically focus on the product and how it is being sold to you. Does the commercial choose to focus on the features of the product, such as price, quality, or value? Or does the commercial focus on the lifestyle associated with the product (how cool you would be if you bought the product)? Why does the commercial try to sell you the product the way it does?

What is going on: Most commercials do not sell products, but instead the lifestyle associated with the product. For example, a product is typically not sold based on rational features such as price, etc. Products are sold through advertising by demonstrating the lifestyle associated with the product. This is especially true with products with little differentiation and with similar characteristics to its competition. In these cases, marketers ask themselves the best way to make people emotionally attached to the product.

Take portable music players as an example. This is a category of product with many selections to choose from thanks to inexpensive manufacturing techniques. There are several hundreds of models to choose from, all of which have similar functionality. But one brand of portable music players stands out from the crowd and leads the market – the Apple iPod line of music players. Is it because this particular product is better, less expensive, or has more functionality? No, but rather this product has clever marketing that appeals to the audience on an emotional level rather than on a rational level. Apple has used this marketing to help sell complementary products that work with the iPod, furthering its appeal.

Chapter 10 – Photography

A picture is worth a thousand words. This is an old cliché, but it is a very true one. Through its unique composition, lighting, framing, subject, and action, just to name a few, a photo has the ability to tell us a story, make us feel a certain emotion, make us act a certain way, and convince us of certain ideas. Photos are all around us – in magazines and newspapers, on billboards and posters, in advertisements of all types, and all over the Internet. This is why we should be aware of the impact photos have on us, and learn to understand the unique language that photography uses to communicate its messages.

Photography has been around since the 1800s, and is considered both an art form and a commercial endeavor. It used to be that photo cameras were for professionals or very wealthy individuals, but in the 1930s Kodak introduced the Brownie camera, which revolutionized photography by allowing anyone to become a photographer. Photography was now for the masses, and millions of photos were taken each year. Today, the digital camera has helped expand photography even further into the mainstream, and the advent of smart phone cameras has put a high quality digital camera in many people's pocket. Thanks to these nearly ubiquitous cameras, it is now just a matter of an hour or so for every million new photos to be brought into the world.

Elements of Photography

Composition

In photography, composition refers to the placement of the elements within the photograph. This includes the following elements:

- **Framing** – how the subject is positioned within the frame. A wider framing takes into account the space around the subject, giving context and a sense of place, while a tighter framing might be used to focus on the subject's emotions or activity. Compare the two photos below – how do the two photos give you a different feeling about the subject and the overall message?

- **Lighting** – The lighting in a photograph can play a major role in how we react emotionally to a photograph. High key lighting leaves no shadows on the subject and feels more open and direct, while low key lighting intentionally accentuates shadows and gives the subject a sense of mystery. Compare the two photos below and think about how each makes you feel.

- **Subject** – The subject of a photo refers to the person or persons presented in the photo, and many characteristics of how the subject is presented can have an effect on how we interpret that photo. For example, who is in the photo and what do they represent? What hints tell us about their situation or personality? What message does the photographer want to send and what emotion do they want you to feel with this photograph? Take a look at the following photograph and think about the intended message.

Migrant Mother, Lange 1

Appendix: Photography-related Learning Activities

ACTIVITY: Camera Angle and Framing

What you need: A recent magazine containing photographs of people (any popular women or men's magazine or teen magazine will do).

How long it takes: This exercise takes about 30 minutes to complete.

What it teaches: This exercise teaches how to recognize how a photo's angle and framing affect our understanding of the subject in the photo.

The activity: Find a variety of magazine photos taken from as many angles as possible – a level angle, a high angle, a low angle, from far away, from up close, etc. Consider how the different angles make you feel about the photos. What did the photographer intend by using that particular angle? How does that angle or framing make you feel about the subject in the photo? Now consider how the photo is framed. Is the subject centered or off to the side? Is the subject framed with just his or her face, or is the shot wider?

What would be the purpose of framing just a person's face instead of the whole body? How does the photograph's message change in either case?

What is going on: A photograph's camera angle and framing tell us a lot about how to feel about the photo and its subject. A low angle aiming upward makes the subject seem larger than life, while a high angle shot from above makes the subject look smaller. A photo taken at the model's height makes the person in the photo seem more accessible, like we are on the same level as them. Framing a photo as a close up typically makes us focus on the subject's emotion, while a wider framing makes us focus on the person's outfit or surroundings. Angle and framing can tell us a lot about the message being sent in a particular photograph.

ACTIVITY: Lighting

What you need: A recent magazine containing photographs of people (any popular women or men's magazine or teen magazine will do).

How long it takes: This exercise takes about 30 minutes to complete.

What it teaches: This exercise helps us understand how lighting in a photograph plays a role in our understanding of the message being sent in that photo.

The activity: Take a look at several magazine photographs that feature people. Examine the lighting in each photo and consider how the lighting was set up (where the lights are coming from), and how the lighting affects the subject in the photo. Does the subject have harsh shadows or barely any shadows? Does the photo seem dark and mysterious, almost unclear, or does it seem bright and open, clearly showing the subject? Why do you think the photographer used that lighting technique in that particular photo? How does the lighting make you feel, and how does it contribute to your overall understanding of the photo?

What is going on: Lighting plays a big role in how we interpret the message in the photo and how we feel about its subject. Harsh shadows can make us feel almost uncomfortable, like the person in the photo is strong, scary, or tough somehow – like the subject has something to hide. Bright lighting with few shadows makes us feel safe, almost happy – like the subject has nothing to hide. Lighting contributes to the tone. Shadows are typically used to infuse "drama", helping add to the seriousness of the photo. This is something you can also examine in a movie – cinematographers are the people who "photograph" a movie, and they play with shadows and light to create a similar effect as we mentioned for photos. Lighting and shadow add another layer of complexity for us to try to understand.

ACTIVITY: The Model

What you need: A recent magazine containing photographs of people (any popular women or men's magazine or teen magazine will do).

How long it takes: This exercise takes about 30 minutes to complete.

What it teaches: This exercise teaches how to recognize how the models and other subjects of photos in magazines are meant to attract our attention and get us to want to read that magazine.

The activity: Examine the front cover model from a recent magazine, or find a variety of photos of models or other people in the magazine and analyze the photos. Is the model in the photo appealing to you? Why or why not? Consider the magazine's target market. Does the person in the photo appeal to people in the magazine's target market? Does the person in the photo look natural, or does the image look like it is too perfect to be from real life?

What is going on: Cover models are chosen to appeal to the magazine's target audience. If the magazine is a fashion magazine aimed towards women, the cover model is likely to be a fashionable woman who somehow makes a woman want to look at her or read about her further.

Most of these models are hired because they meet some kind of stereotype. In a travel magazine, you are likely to see people on the cover having fun: smiling, laughing, and playing. The models will not look angry or sad, because people reading travel magazines want to see where other people are having fun, not having a bad vacation.

Magazine publishers also use airbrushing and retouching tools like Adobe Photoshop to smooth out any imperfections in the photo, making the model look “perfect.” People sometimes try to look like the person on the cover of a magazine, but they become disappointed because they cannot attain the perfection that Photoshop can create for us.

ACTIVITY: The Big Idea

What you need: A recent magazine containing a variety of different photographs, as well as several artistic photos pulled from art gallery or museum websites.

How long it takes: This exercise takes about 30 minutes to complete.

What it teaches: This exercise teaches how to recognize a photograph’s main idea, and how that main idea is conveyed through the various elements of photography.

The activity: Examine the photograph you have chosen to work with. What is the photograph's central concept? What is the big idea that the photographer is trying to convey? What elements of photography help tell you about the big idea (i.e. Shadows and lighting, framing and camera angle, the subject of the photo, etc.)? What message did the photographer intend to send to the viewer?

What is going on: Photographs do not use words to tell us what they are trying to convey, but instead rely on visuals to tell us what we are supposed to understand about them. Photographers can combine all of the elements of photography to convey a specific meaning from the photo. Examining popular photography from magazines helps us understand the types of photos that we are exposed most to, while artistic photos can help us understand the more subtle aspects of photography.

Chapter 11 – Advertising

Advertising is the way that companies sell us their products through the media, and it is all around us. When we think about advertising, we think about ads on television or in a magazine, but these days we can find advertising anywhere traditional media exists (in a movie theater before the movie, on the radio, on a billboard on the street), in new places that have popped up more recently (on almost every website we visit, in smartphone and tablet video games), and in places that have not traditionally been known to have advertising (inside the movie or TV show in the form of product placement, at sporting and entertainment events). In addition to these areas that we can be exposed to advertising, there are subtle advertisements in the form of brand logos on nearly every product we use.

With so much advertising, it is no wonder that so much of it goes under our radar and we just miss it. By not recognizing each time we are exposed to an advertising message, we allow that message to affect us in subtle ways. Not only are we more likely to purchase a product that we would not otherwise considering purchasing, but we also buy into the lifestyles or stereotypes found in advertisements. Whether we recognize it or not, we are affected by the depictions of “normal life” in advertisements. I will talk more about this in just a moment, but it is obvious that advertising affects us deeply, and we should learn to recognize the messages in them.

What is advertising?

To begin, we should explain the meaning of advertising. Although there may be a variety of ways of explaining advertising as a concept, the simplest way to explain it is to say that advertising is *sales through media.*

Before modern advertising (on TV, radio, and in print), we may have gone into a car dealership to buy a car and the salesperson may have explained the features and benefits of the car to the customer. The features are actual physical details of the car – it is 10 feet long, can go 60 miles per hour, and uses a gallon of gas for every 10 miles (remember, we’re talking about a long time ago!). The benefits are how the features will help the customer in some way – the car can fit the whole family, can reach its destination in less time than a horse buggy, and runs on inexpensive fuel. The salesperson would try to convince you that these features and benefits would fit you and you would buy the car.

Along comes advertising in print and on radio, and the first ads mimicked almost exactly the sales pitch by a live salesperson.

Colors That Match the Season's Mode

AMONG the features of the Ford car is the privilege of selecting from a variety of beautiful colors. These colors are rich in tone and are changed at frequent intervals, in keeping with the season's mode. Frequently you will find that one of Fashion's newest shades, or a harmonious blending of it, is available also in the Ford car.

With reasonable care, the smooth, gleaming finish of the Ford car as it comes fresh from the showrooms may be maintained for a long period. The pyroxylin lacquer is not affected by heat or cold and is easily polished to a shimmering luster. The Rustless Steel used for the radiator shell, hub caps, cowl finish strip and other exterior metal parts is an additional assurance of enduring worth and permanent beauty. Throughout the life of the car it will not scale, tarnish or corrode.

Ford

Ford ad from the 1930s 1

This Ford advertisement from the 1930s lists the car's features and benefits in long form, and combines it with an image of the car itself to show the customer what it looks like and how it could be useful.

As advertising evolved over the years, ads became more sophisticated and began focusing more on benefits than on features. Today, most advertising focuses almost exclusively on the product's benefits than features.

A classic example is with advertising for laundry detergent. Traditionally, most purchasers of laundry detergent for a household with children have been women – moms (although this is changing as many dads are choosing to be responsible for most of the house chores). If we think of the features of laundry detergent, we could say that it is either powder or liquid, contains bleach or does not, and protects colors over many washes or does not. The benefits might be that the detergent gets white clothing very white, or that it does a good job of removing stains. By focusing on the benefits rather than on the features, and by featuring mini-stories of moms getting their family's clothing nicely clean, laundry detergent manufacturers are really sending this message to moms: "if you use our detergent, your whites will stay white, your stains will come out, and your family will be happy."

Vintage 1946 advertisement for Tide

In essence, advertisers are no longer selling products – they are selling a feeling or an emotion. This is especially true for products that have very little differentiation. For example, can you really tell the difference between a Pepsi and a Coca-Cola, especially if you do not drink soda too often? Think about how many times you have said "no" in a restaurant when you asked for a Coke and they say "Is Pepsi ok?" Probably not too many times. But when they have a choice (like at the super market), consumers who are loyal to a particular soda brand will only look for their favorite soda brand and ignore all others, even if there is a sale for the other brand. This is typically because the brand speaks to them somehow – the commercials have made them feel an emotional connection that makes them want to buy a particular product over any other.

Elements of Advertising

Keeping in mind that our definition of advertising is sales through media, let us think for a moment to consider how a salesperson might sell you a product. Have you ever been at the mall and someone approaches you from one of the shops in a cart and they want you to try a lotion for your hands? Most people I know have been in this situation. You are walking through the mall, minding your own business, when someone approaches you and says "Hi, how are you? Can I give you some free lotion to try?" Depending on whether you are interested in lotion at the moment (or if you like free things!), you may say ok and let the salesperson give you some hand lotion. The lotion goes on smooth on your hands, and it feels good as you rub it in your hands. The salesperson tells you to smell it. You smell it and it smells wonderful. Now, the salesperson tells you that you can have a bottle for $20. You think about it and say, "Well, I'm not sure," so they say they will give you two bottles for $30 if you buy it now.

The story I just told is an example of the sales process. Salespeople are taught early in their careers about the sales process by using an acronym: A-I-D-A – Attention, Interest, Desire, Action. First, the salesperson should get the customer's attention. They do this by greeting you and offering you free lotion. They then get you interested in the product. They give you some to try and ask you to rub it on your hands. They may tell you it will make your hands soft, or that the ingredients are organic. Once you are interested, they make you desire the product. The lotion feels great in your hands and it smells great. Finally, they want you to take action by telling you the price and asking you to buy one or two bottles.

Believe it or not, advertising uses this same technique to sell you a product or service. Try looking at an advertisement in a magazine or newspaper, or turn on the TV or radio and wait for the commercials, then try to figure out 1) how do they get your attention, 2) how do they get you interested in the product, 3) how do they make you desire the product, and 4) how do they tell you how to take action to buy the product. Every good advertisement will contain these four steps of the sales process, and once you know this you can start to look at advertising more critically.

Advertising Appeals

Advertising attempts to appeal to consumers at different levels. Sometimes the appeal is rational. An advertisement for a laptop might tell you the specifications – CPU speed, amount of memory, screen size. Laptop ads are usually rational because we need specific things in a laptop to do the things we want to do – homework, games, etc. The ads for other products can sometime be irrational. An advertisement for a car might focus more on how much fun you are going to have with it rather than how big the engine is or what kind of gas you need to use with it. As you may have already realized, *rational ads focus on features, while irrational ads focus on benefits.* Here is a list of rational and irrational appeals in advertisements.

- Rational – Focuses on Practical Use
    - **Form –** Is it designed to meet my needs?
    - **Function –** Does it do what I need it to do?
    - **Price –** How much does it cost?

- Irrational – Based on Emotions
    - **Personal** – How will this make me feel?
    - **Social** – How will others see me if I buy this?
    - **Fear** – What will I lose if I do not get this?
    - **Humor** – Causes a laugh

- **Sex –** Will this help me find a partner?
- **Music –** Gets attention, creates connection.
- **Scarcity –** Act now, before it is gone!

Maslow's Hierarchy of Needs

Advertisements try to fill a need in the consumer's life – either a practical need or an emotional need. A scientist named Abraham Maslow once explored how and why we need things. He created a hierarchy that explains how needs are met in our lives. First, we need to fulfill our basic needs (food, water, sleep), and then we can move up his pyramid to fulfill more needs.

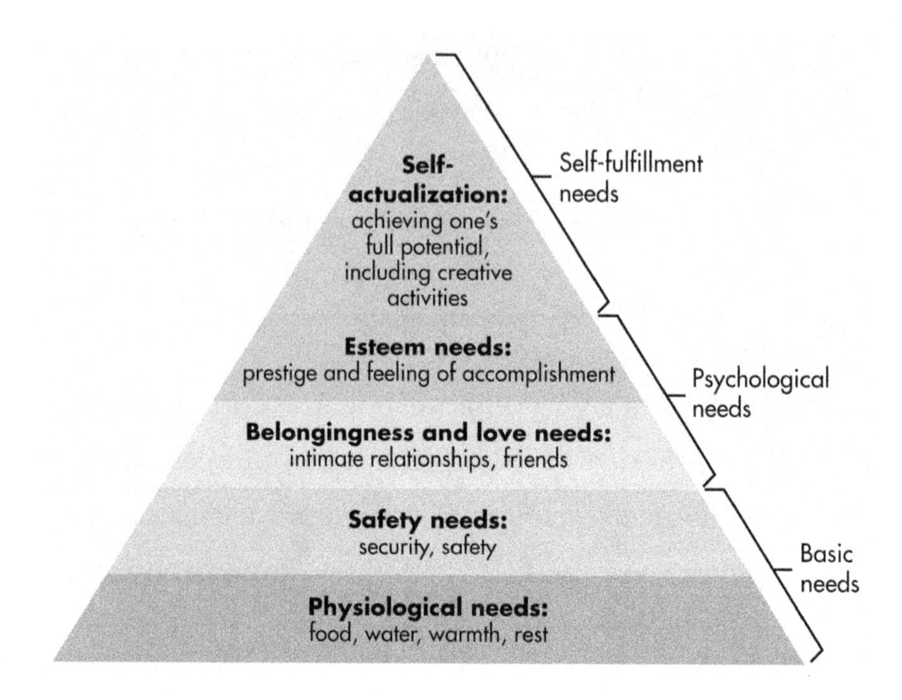

Maslow's Hierarchy of Needs

Consider how advertisers use this hierarchy of needs to sell us products. Here are just some examples of advertisements appealing to different needs.

Michelin ad appealing to our need for safety.

Coca-Cola ad appealing to our need for belonging.

BMW ad appealing to our need for prestige

University of Phoenix ad appealing to our need for self-realization.

How does advertising affect us?

Advertising affects us at a deep psychological level, and it is worth exploring these affects to better understand them. Most major effects of advertising can be categorized in one of two groups: consumerism affects and stereotyping affects.

Consumerism

A common criticism of advertising is that it helps contribute to increases in consumerism. Advertising may lead us to buy things we do not neat, to accumulate debt by spending money we do not have, to give us feelings of inadequacy – we constantly think we do not have enough, and to “keep up with the Joneses” – we always want more.

Stereotyping

Since advertising tries to tell us so much in such little space or time (a half-page print ad, a 30-second TV or radio commercial), advertising frequently uses stereotypes – characters or situations portrayed in a simplified, often negative way – to give us their messages quickly. For example, if you are an advertiser selling computers to engineers, you may portray an engineer in the ad so that other engineers can quickly associate with that person. But what kinds of simple characteristics will quickly tell the audience “this is a computer engineer”? The character is typically male, poorly styled with a plain shirt, and wears geeky glasses. When we see this character, we typically think about all of the characteristics that go along with the stereotype.

Still from a CDW TV commercial featuring Charles Barkley

The obvious criticism regarding stereotypes is that they present a distorted view of the world. Not all computer engineers dress like this, they are not all male, and not all of them are straight-A students. The stereotype gives us an unrealistic perspective on what it is to be a computer engineer, and this affects society on a deep level. When a woman experiences this stereotype over and over again throughout her youth, she might decide that she is not meant for a career in computers because she does not “fit the mold.” Can you think of any other harmful and unrealistic stereotypes we see in advertising?

Now that you have a basic understanding about advertising, the following activities will help you further understand how ads work and how they affect us.

Appendix: Advertising-based Learning Activities

ACTIVITY: Advertising and Stereotypes

A long time ago, companies did something very strange with how they advertise their products. Instead of selling us their products and services by telling us about their features (the characteristics of the product that makes it better than another product), and benefits (how those characteristics will help us live better lives), companies began selling us on the lifestyle associated with the product or service. Instead of saying, "this laundry detergent will make your clothing the cleanest", they began saying "this laundry detergent will make you happier." Companies moved away from using announcers and images of their products to using characters – people that reflected the product's target market. For example, that laundry detergent ad might feature a mother with two children. Instead of the ad saying "your children's clothing will be clean," the ad now said "your children will love you more." Who does not want to hear that their children will love them more? This is a very powerful and subtle message, and these techniques are still used today.

Beer commercials – mostly still targeted towards men – do not sell beer; they sell the lifestyle of what society sees as a man's lifestyle, with "beautiful" women and freedom from life's responsibilities. Toys are sold as a way to be liked by others, not as a way to have fun. Advertisers know what pushes our buttons, and they exploit them.

To be fair to advertisers, they are not always aware they are selling us a lifestyle rather than a product or service. People in the advertising industry have been taught to sell products to consumers based on their needs and desires. Along the way, advertisers discovered that selling to consumers' emotional needs, rather than to their practical needs, was a great way to increase sales.

A number of problems exist with this method of selling products, but we will focus on just one: advertising leading to stereotyping of the audience.

Companies do not sell products to everyone. They sell their products to specific people – their target market.

This is the reason why if you are a woman, you will almost never see an ad for men's shaving cream in media outlets aimed specifically toward women. It is because the company advertising the men's shaving cream understands what types of media men consume, and what type of media women consume. Although there is some overlap, the company knows that men typically consume media that society deems appropriate for men. For example, it is a typical assumption that men like to watch sports. So advertisers place their ads for products aimed towards men during sporting events.

This "typical" assumption is where we enter into the area of stereotyping. In order to market specific products to specific people, companies assume certain things about the people they are selling to, and then use those assumptions to try to attract that customer. For example, with the men's shaving cream, the company will attempt to differentiate the shaving cream used for men's faces, as opposed to the shaving cream used for women's legs. By doing this, they must explicitly demonstrate that this shaving cream is for men, and not women, although for the most part shaving cream is shaving cream!

Instead of displaying “this is only for men!” in large letters in the advertisement, advertisers rely on stereotypes to indicate the preferred market for the product. In our example of men’s shaving cream, the advertisers may show a character of a “typical” man with a beard after he has taken a shower. He reaches for his shaving cream, and it is of course the brand being advertised.

In order to get men interested in the advertisement, the company may use an actor that society deems attractive, rather than an actor that society deems disgusting. So by showing us an “attractive” man and depicting him as “typical”, our image of what a man should look like is formed. This leads to stereotyping of what a man should look like, how a man should act, and of course, what product a man should shave with.

Over time, and with enough stereotypes depicted, a company will be able to sell its brand to loyal customers, but at a heavy cost in terms of our perceptions about people.

The following exercises will help us better understand advertising, and the ways in which advertising affects us.

ACTIVITY: Brands

What you need: A variety of brand logos that can be found on the internet. Perform a search for a company's logo and remove any words that may be present.

How long it takes: This exercise takes approximately 30 minutes to compete.

What it teaches: This exercise teachings how powerful brands and logos can be, and how they influence our buying decisions.

The activity: Take a look at the brand logo you have chosen to use. Consider why the company chose this image as their logo. What does the logo represent? Who is the company's target market and how is this logo supposed to appeal to them? What are the feelings you have about this company, and how does the logo relate to those feelings? Can you name some of this company's competitors? How are this company's products different than the competitor's? Does this company use some special technology or patented feature that makes it different from the others? Are the products for this company better or worse than those of the competitors, and how do you know? What is the lifestyle that the company is selling?

What is going on: Brands are most powerful for products that are commodities (a commodity is a type of product that has many competitors and so must be sold in many cases based on low price, for example, shoes, soda, clothing, and cars). Brands help make a product seem different than a competitor's, meaning that a company with a strong brand can charge more for their product, even though all of the products in that category are practically the same. Companies use logos to help them establish their brand visually in the customer's mind. If when you see an image of an apple with a bite taken out of it, you think of a particular computer and phone company, then Apple has succeeded in associating that logo with their company. It also makes you more likely to buy an Apple product rather than a competing product, even though all of the product categories that Apple competes in has products of similar quality. Apple can charge you a higher price for their products because you are willing to pay more based on your idea that Apple's products are superior in some way. In fact, most of the smartphones and computers that Apple sells are made in the same factories as competing products!

ACTIVITY: Intended Audiences and Messages

What you need: Find some humorous television ads on YouTube – maybe search for "funny commercials" to find some suitable choices.

How long it takes: This exercise takes approximately 30 minutes.

What it teaches: This exercise teaches how to interpret the messages in advertisements, and to realize that ads have an intended audience with certain expectations.

The activity: Watch the ads and ask these questions: Who is the intended audience for the ad? How do you know? What makes the advertisement funny? Are the characters funny? Are the characters in a funny situation? How does the ad portray the characters? Are the portrayals positive or negative? If the character portrayals are negative, ask yourself why negative portrayals are funny. What is the message being sent? Ask yourself how someone different than you might interpret this commercial. If you find it funny, could someone else find it in bad taste or offensive? If you do not find the commercial funny, ask yourself why the advertiser thought the commercial would be funny.

What is going on: TV commercials, just like other types of advertisements and even other types of media, are aimed towards specific groups of people (target markets). People in these groups share common characteristics and common life stories. This makes it easy for companies to make commercials intended to appeal to certain people by tapping into their stories and culture. As an example, society seems to be ok to tease and mock people who are overweight (if you disagree, take a look at the main actors in the most successful comedy movies over the past ten years). Although this behavior seems wrong, many people may find it funny if an overweight character on TV is doing something silly.

An advertisement might exploit this fact for humor in order to appeal to people who find this type of humor funny. They may sell some products based on this ad, but the cost is the negative portrayals of people who are overweight. Millions struggle with their weight, and this is no laughing matter when it concerns issues of health and body image issues, but having an overweight character doing something funny for 30 seconds often seems like an easy way for advertisers to get a laugh, and in turn create a positive association with their product.

ACTIVITY: Product Placements

What you need: An episode of a recent reality television show or prime-time comedy or drama.

How long it takes: This exercise takes 30 minutes, in addition to the time to watch the television episode. For a 30-minute episode, this exercise take one hour to complete.

What it teaches: This exercise teaches how to recognize hidden advertisements called "product placements" in television shows.

The activity: Watch an episode of a recent television reality show or prime-time comedy or drama. Try to not pay attention to the story as much, but focus on the things you see and hear on screen. Can you see any company logos, or real products being used or talked about? Why do you think those products or brands appeared in the show? Do you think the brand owner paid to have their product or brand in the show, or do you think that maybe it was just a coincidence that the product appeared there? If you think the company paid money to have the product placed in the show, why do you think the company thought it was a good idea to do so? Why do you think, from the advertiser's point of view, placing the product in the show itself is better than having a 30-second commercial play during the show?

What is going on: Advertisers are always trying to find new ways to make sure the audience knows about their products. Not only do advertisers pay the show's producer to have their products appear and even play a role in the television show, but the show producers actually have people working to attract more of these types of advertisements. Product placement happens for two main reasons. The first reason is because a lot of people use digital video recorders today, so they get to record a show and then fast forward through the commercials. If the product appears in the show, advertisers know you will not fast forward the show itself, so you will be forced to see this "ad." The second main reason is because advertisers know that, if your favorite character on the show uses a specific product, you will have a positive response to the product. Essentially, if your favorite character drinks Pepsi, that company hopes you might try Pepsi and like it as well.

ACTIVITY: Text in Print Advertisements

What you need: Several print advertisements cut out of a newspaper or magazine.

How long it takes: This exercise takes approximately 30 minutes.

What it teaches: This exercise teaches how to interpret the meaning of the text in a print advertisement.

The activity: Cut out several advertisements from a magazine or newspaper. Examine the ad and consider the following: Who is the intended audience for the advertisement? What elements of the ad tell you about its intended audience? Maybe the text is of a certain color, or the writing tells you who the ad is aimed towards. After reading the ad, consider what the text is really saying. Read between the lines and think about the implied meaning. The purpose of the words in a print advertisement is to evoke an emotion. How does the text make you feel? If there is a headline (usually the message in the largest font), how does it grab your attention? How does the text relate to the images? What does the main text tell us about the product? Does the main text tell us anything about the product itself (like features and benefits), or does the ad prefer to sell the reader on the lifestyle associated with the product? Finish this sentence according to the advertisement's real message: "If you buy this product, your life will be better because... "

What is going on: The text in each advertisement was carefully crafted to convey a particular message about the product. Typically advertisements sell products by engaging the audience emotionally instead of rationally. It is important to interpret the text's deep meaning – the subtext – and not take it literally. Remember, an advertisement's purpose is to give you a positive association with the product. This is done by relating how the product will make your life better if you buy it.

ACTIVITY: Images in Print Advertisements

What you need: Several print advertisements cut out of a newspaper or magazine.

How long it takes: This exercise takes approximately 30 minutes.

What it teaches: This exercise teaches how to interpret the meaning of the images in a print advertisement.

The activity: Cut out several advertisements from a magazine or newspaper. What do the images tell you what the ad is about? Are there people in the ad, or is it just the product? If there are people in the ad, why were those people chosen as the models for the ad? Does the photo depict a certain lifestyle associated with the product? What kind of emotional response does the photo have on you? How does it make you feel? How did the ad creator think the photo would get your attention as a consumer? What is the hidden meaning or subtext in the photo? Are there any stereotypes present in the ad? What is the message that the photo is sending? Finish this sentence according to the advertisement's real message: "If you buy this product, your life will be better because... "

What is going on: Pictures are worth a thousand words, and this is especially true for print advertisements. Since print ads do not have motion or sound like television advertisements, they rely on just text and images to sell the product to the reader. The photo used in a print advertisement usually packs a lot of meaning in a small amount of space. Advertisers know that they have one or two seconds to grab your attention and get you to read further, so the photo they choose is critical. The photo should make you stop what you are doing (probably flipping pages), and make you pay attention. This is why photos in advertisements are often over the top, or feature something (or someone) attractive enough to keep your attention. Since they have only a second or two, advertisers often use stereotypes to relate to the reader.

ACTIVITY: Intended Audience and Impact

What you need: Several print advertisements cut out of a newspaper or magazine.

How long it takes: This exercise takes approximately 30 minutes.

What it teaches: This exercise teaches how to discover an advertisement's intended audience, and how the advertisement is meant to have an impact on that audience.

The activity: Cut out several advertisements from a magazine or newspaper. Just by looking at the ad, can you tell who the ad's intended audience is? If so, what elements in the ad tell you about the intended audience? What magazine or newspaper did this ad appear in, and does that give you any clue about the intended audience? After you have an idea of who the ad is trying to target, consider how someone different from the target audience might interpret the ad. Does the ad contain any stereotypes that the intended audience could relate to or find familiar? Would someone from a different gender, age group, race, or income level find the ad appealing, offensive, or maybe be indifferent? What values does the ad contain? Is it young, hip, mature, playful, and exciting? Why did the advertiser choose to publish this advertisement where they did? What do you think is the intended impact of this advertisement?

What is going on: Discovering an ad's intended audience is critical for understanding the advertisement itself. Advertisers try to appeal to specific audiences in their ads, and they embed messages that the intended audience will understand. For example, an ad aimed towards teens might have text in it that claims "better than your first kiss," or something similar that this group would find appealing. There are at least two problems with this. First, advertisers do not know each of the people who will see this ad personally, so they need to generalize the message by incorporating stereotypes. The stereotype in the example above is that teens value their first kiss above all else. This is obviously a shallow and generalized representation of teenagers, but advertisers know this message will appeal to many teens, if not all of them. This type of generalization, as experienced thousands of times over in our lives, creates the stereotype that teens should value their first kiss above all else, and if they do not, then there is something wrong with them. The second issue with using these types of generalizations is that they make it difficult to understand the message if you are not a part of the target audience. Using our above example again, someone in their twenties will be turned off by the pandering to teenagers, especially since that person is past that point in their lives. Ads that are too specific in their targeting and in their stereotypical portrayals also have the potential effect of offending people outside of the main target audience. Advertisements for products aimed toward men are a great example of this. These types of advertisements typically contain offensive (or at minimum, hurtful) portrayals of women for the benefit of selling products to the male audience. Again depicting stereotypical situations between men and women, over time these repeated depictions create barriers and animosity between men and women.

ACTIVITY: Ads All Around Us

What you need: An average room, classroom, or workspace.

How long it takes: This exercise takes about 20 minutes to complete.

What it teaches: This exercise teaches how to recognize and be aware of the multitude of advertisements and promotions that exist in our everyday environments.

The activity: Take a look around the room for about one minute. How many different brand logos can you spot? This includes the logos on t-shirts, water bottles, shoes, backpacks, windows, anything. Write down the different logos you see. After a minute, add up the number of logos you saw. Now take another minute and try to find more logos. Try doing this activity with a friend or with a group of people. See who finds more brands and logos in one minute, and who notices more brands and logos in two minutes. See if others spotted more or different brands than you.

What is going on: Brand logos are all around us, and although they are not typically considered advertisements, they certainly are. After all, are you more likely to buy a certain brand of phone or shoe if someone around you uses that brand? Studies show that you are. These brand logos hide in plain sight, and we do not notice them because we are not looking for them. The end result is that we end up internalizing the brands and the ideas behind them without even realizing it. Just because an advertisement is not on television or in a magazine, it does not mean that the ad does not affect us. We should be aware of all of the advertisements around us in order to better understand how we are influenced to buy products, and this includes the ads disguised as everyday objects.

ACTIVITY: Design a Product Package

What you need: A piece of paper and a writing instrument for each person participating in this exercise.

How long it takes: This exercise can take up to an hour or longer to complete.

What it teaches: This exercise teaches us to recognize how powerful product packaging can be, and how that power can influence us to buy the product.

The activity: Choose a product that can be purchased at a retail store and design a package for it. First, consider who you think the target audience is for this product. Then, design a package that appeals to that audience. Draw the artwork based on your target audience's age, gender, income level, location, and interests. Be ready to explain why you think your product package will appeal to the intended target market.

What is going on: Many of the products that we purchase exist in a category with many competitors. When trying to sell us a particular product, the company selling it needs to consider what makes the product special, or at least why should we buy this product instead of a competing product. Many times, we make our decisions at the last moment based on a product's packaging. Consider breakfast cereal; most breakfast cereals are very similar, and there are many type of "flakes," "oats," and "puffy corn" cereals. What makes them different? The difference is usually the packaging, and a strong recognizable cereal package can demand a higher price. The bigger question is, why do we buy the products we buy? Sometimes the reason is not due to a rational explanation, but rather because of an emotional response.

Chapter 12: Fake News and Other Media Tricks

The media, especially commercial media, as well as media figures, especially those who are considered "news makers" (ie. Political leaders) have tools at their disposal to manipulate the media, and therefore manipulate what we experience and how we think about the world. This is done through the news mainly, but can also be in any media form, including advertising and short- or long-form video or audio content.

The more we understand these techniques, the better equipped we are to recognize when they are being used and we can defend against them. We do this by first being aware that they exist, second that we are being manipulated, and third we can choose to accept or reject that media message based on our values.

The media manipulation techniques we will learn about in this section have grown in popularity and have seen an uptick in use, especially since the presidential election cycle of 2016.

Fake News

Fake News has been a phrase that has been in existence for a long time before the current era. We can go back to the newspapers of William Randolph Hearst, and to the concept of yellow journalism. In this era of the 1920s and 1930s, Fake News was considered just that – news that was false, manufactured, devoid of facts, or deceitful. Typically these types of news stories were meant to be sensational in nature and with a primary goal of making money. Today we may consider a publication like The National Enquirer as a prime example. But digging a little deeper, we may see any gossip magazine or website as sensational and with the sole function of making money.

Today's version of Fake News is much different than that of yellow journalism. What today we consider Fake News is when a politician or a political aide calls anything they disagree with Fake News. For example, President Donald Trump has used the term in response to accusations of any kind. Whenever he is accused of something, his response is "Fake News!," which immediately throws into doubt the truthfulness of the accusation or news source.

Calling something Fake News muddies the waters of media clarity and confuses people receiving the message, making them focus on the Fake News argument rather than on the facts of the revelation or the accusation.

At times, President Trump has said something was Fake News, even after absolute proof (a video, and audio recording, a document) exists. Again, this shifts the focus to the denial rather than the accusation. It also shuts down any discussion about the issue, since it signals from the sender that the issue will no longer be addressed. This limits the media's ability to bring us the truth, since the participants are denying and dismissing the claim. The media is either forced to continue a largely fruitless line of investigation, or move on to something else that will capture the audience's attention.

As an example, imagine if a video surfaces of a politician saying something truly disturbing. It is right there in the video and we know it exists. The politician comes out an calls the video (or perhaps the consequences of the video) Fake News. Suddenly the media is on the defensive, needing to show that video again to prove it is not Fake News as the politician continues to claim it is Fake News. On the evening news, the anchor may just show a clip of the video evidence, and then the politician's denial. The story usually dies right then and there, since the editors of the news do not want to continue playing back a denial, since this does not earn ratings. The public becomes tired of the back and forth and the news organization moves to the next story.

The problem is that, after a while, the news media comes to expect that when the politician calls a story Fake News, the story is good for one news cycle (one day), and then they must move on to the next story to continue entertaining audiences. Politicians understand this power to stifle the news media, and they now use it at every turn.

(https://en.wikipedia.org/wiki/Fake_news)

Alternative Facts

The term Alternative Facts came into being after it was coined on live air by President Trump's advisor, Kellyanne Conway when responding to then press secretary Sean Spicer's response regarding the number of people who attended the President's inauguration. Chuck Todd from NBC's Meet the Press, pressed Conway on why the President sent out Spicer on his first address to the nation and to "utter a provable falsehood," and Conway responded that Spicer gave Alternative Facts about the number of people at the inauguration. Todd responded, "alternative facts are not facts, they're falsehoods."

The problem here is obvious, if someone can say any falsehood, present it as fact (clearly not indicating that it is an opinion, and therefore open to argument), then the idea of a fact is weakened and has little meaning after time. In the original case of Sean Spicer, he gave a specific number of people who attended the President's inauguration. He never said "a lot," or "plenty," or "a huge amount of people," but instead stated a number that was nowhere close to the actual number of people who attended.

Going beyond an issue that, admittedly, has no real consequence to anyone, and towards issues that do have consequences. Can the public trust someone who makes up their own facts and claims they are simply "Alternative?" We can adapt this to the coronavirus crisis. How many people were tested in mid-June of 2020? At a rally in Tulsa, Oklahoma, the

President said there were so many cases, that testing should be "slowed down." This would have the effect of having an unreliable accounting of how many people are affected with the virus. When there are no official numbers, you can make any number sound true. A day later, when the President was asked about if he was serious about slowing down testing, he said the numbers on tests were good, and that the United States had the most cases globally because the United States tests more than any other country. These too, were Alternative Facts.

This issue comes down to trust. Trust in our leaders, trust in the media, trust in any system that is being questioned. A democracy relies on facts for the people to make informed decisions about important matters. Once that trust is lost, it is very difficult to regain.

(https://en.wikipedia.org/wiki/Alternative_facts)

Whataboutism has been around for decades, and was an argument technique used by political propagandists during the Cold War years between the United States and the Soviet Union. In essence, Whataboutism attempts to discredit and opponent's claim or position by charging them with hypocrisy or favoritism without directly refuting or disproving their argument. (Wikipedia)

An example of Whataboutism is when a politician (or any public figure) is asked about something they did that is wrong, and instead of responding to the charge against them, they respond "well, what about this that you (or your side) did?" They are not directly responding to the claim made against them, but instead responding with a non-reponse and a counter-argument accusing the other side of doing something, whether it be similar or not.

For a more concrete example, we go again to Kellyanne Conway, President Trump's advisor. During her interview with Chuck Todd in which she coined the phrase Alternative Facts, after being pushed about her use of the term, her eventual response was "Well, what about President Obama..." Over the years, we have heard from many political leaders, their advisors, and spokespeople have used Whataboutism as a way to deflect an argument they know they cannot win and so they choose to change the subject against the other side.

Whataboutism is dangerous when used in the media because it dilutes an argument or situation by attempting to make the audience focus on another topic. The best defense against Whataboutism in the media is asking yourself, "did the person being asked the question actually answer the question?" If you start a line of questioning at topic (A) and end up with answers from topic (Z), you know you are being steered away from the actual purpose of the discussion or interview.

Another problem with Whataboutism is the limited time the media has for an interview. If a television show only has a guest for one segment (5-7 minutes), the interviewer can be stonewalled by the guest by responding with Whataboutisms until the clock runs out. This steers the conversation off course and gets away from the answers to the questions the public wants to know about. So the public does not get the full story and instead deflected into another direction.

(https://en.wikipedia.org/wiki/Whataboutism)

Gaslighting

Gaslighting is a type of manipulation in which a person to a group covertly sows seeds of doubt in another person or group, making them question their own memory, perception, judgement, often evoking in them cognitive dissonance and other changes including low self-esteem. Using denial, misdirection, contradiction, and misinformation, gaslighting involves attempts to destabilize the victim and delegitimize the victim's beliefs. Instances can range from the denial by an abuser that previous abusive incidents occurred, to the staging of bizarre events by the abuser with the intention of disorienting the victim. (Wikipedia)

The term comes from a play and film adaptations called "Gas Light," in which a husband tries to manipulate his wife into thinking she is insane by challenging her version of reality. Remember, that "truth" is subjective, and what we believe are facts are sometimes (incorrectly) open to interpretation. In the media, there is a phrase that says, “don’t pee on me and tell me it’s raining!” This is the essence of gaslighting.

President Trump is an expert gaslighter. In June 2020, after stoking racial tensions during the George Floyd protests, he re-tweeted a video of a man who yelled “white power,” as he rolled by in a golf cart. After having re-tweeted other racist dog whistles (extremely racist to those who get the reference, but otherwise going unnoticed) in the past, the media was up in arms about the re-tweet. The thought was, how could the President of the United States brazenly re-tweet a video of obvious and disgusting white supremacy? When the outrage hit the news, the President deleted the re-tweet and then told the media he hadn’t heard what the person was saying in the video (though the offensive phrase as prominent and being yelled clearly through the video). This is gaslighting – “no, I would never do that in good conscious, you must be insane to think I did that on purpose!” or “I find it offensive that you would even believe I would do that if I knew what it meant… how dare you!”

Often times, an expert gaslighter will turn it around onto the person or group who pointed out the error. Despite President Trump's actions, he claims, "no one has done more for black people than I have. It is offensive to think so." Trump once said, "What you're seeing and what you're reading is not happening." Trump's attorney and former New York mayor, Rudy Giuliani, once said "Truth isn't truth." These are all examples of gaslighting.

(https://en.wikipedia.org/wiki/Gaslighting)

Alarmism

Alarmism is excessive or exaggerated alarm about a real or imagined threat, such as the increases in deaths from an infectious disease. In the news media, alarmism can be a form of yellow journalism where reports sensationalize a story to exaggerate small risks. (Wikipedia)

An example is the pandemic of 2020. The news media used the same language of *breaking news: coronavirus cases rising at this hour* whether cases were up by 10 or by 10,000. There is an appropriate time to sound the alarm, but to do it daily in order to get ratings is where the idea of alarmism comes in.

Another example from the same period (May 2020) is when protestors marching in support of George Floyd and against the police's use of excessive force. The news cameras left the peaceful protests to show the one department store being looted, then used language like, *peaceful protests have turned violent, have lead to looting,* making it appear that all protestors were looting which was not the case.

Alarmism is one way the media sensationalizes the events happening around the world, and focuses on the worst aspects of an event when they are reporting. A rioter throwing rocks at a police car or lighting wood on fire in the middle of the street is sensational, and will get viewers to continue watching, which is why the news media kept repeating these images and not of the peaceful protests. The result is that viewers become alarmed, panic sets in, and fear takes over. When the audience becomes fearful of what they see in a video, they gain a negative view of the world and of the people in the video.

If the news media overuses alarmism, it can lose its meaning. For example, the constant us of the term "breaking news" with red text and a powerful short piece of music has lost it's meaning with audiences. It used to be that "breaking news" was reserved for important news that was just happening at that moment, but now the term is used for untimely stories (stories that happened earlier in the day or the day before), but also for minor updates to past stories, or even for news that is not really that important. The news media wants to make it seem that there is always something bad happening in the world so that you will continue watching, but often this leaves the viewer alarmed about the state of the world, or worse, numb to the events happening in the world.

(https://en.wikipedia.org/wiki/Alarmism)

Blatant Bias

We've studied bias in the news media. In fact, we discovered that it is impossible not to have a bias, since we are all human and we all bring our own ideas to a situation. The hidden bias occurs when our biases are very subtle (the use of one word over another, the fact that a story even runs at a news outlet). These biases are everywhere. However, there is another, more dangerous bias – blatant bias. This is when the media strongly and obviously chooses to show one point of view strongly over a different point of view, without shame or reservation that they are taking that view.

Two prime examples of blatant bias are the news networks Fox News and MSNBC. Both have a blatant bias, the first toward conservative points of view, and the second toward liberal points of view. Neither specifically shouts "we are conservative" or "we are liberal" but instead Fox News always takes its talking points from a conservative point of view in order to push forward a conservative agenda, and MSNBC always takes its talking points from a liberal point of view in order to push forward a liberal agenda. They cite sources from other like-minded media, they only invite guests who agree with their point of view. If they do invite guests "from the other side," they are often either sympathetic to the outlet's point of view, or else they are a "straw man," a guest who holds a weak or easily defeatable position.

The consequences of blatant bias are many, but primarily and most importantly, the audience who is exposed to this blatant bias is typically said to be in a "bubble" of information. They keep hearing the same one-sided arguments and rarely, if ever, hear the other side. This causes a cognitive dissonance between the real world, and the world inside the bubble. Inside the bubble, everyone on the other side is stupid, horrible, deplorable, etc., and this serves solely to divide viewers and readers. By simply acknowledging that there is a blatant bias in the media you consume, you can allow yourself to be open to other opinions and points of view. Better yet, try finding media sources that do not rely so much on opinion and analysis, as they do on facts and provable statements.

(https://en.wikipedia.org/wiki/Media_bias)

Victim Blaming

Victim blaming occurs when the victim of a crime or any wrongful act is held entirely or partially at fault for the harm that befell them. The study of victimology seeks to mitigate the prejudice against victims, and the perception that victims are in any way responsible for the actions of offenders. There is historical and current prejudice against the victims of domestic violence and sex crimes, such as the greater tendency to blame victims of rape than victims of robbery if victims and perpetrators knew each other prior to the commission of the crime. (Wikipedia)

As an example, an article highlighting rape in the Philippines called *Victim-blaming: Why survivors of sexual violence won't come forward*, by Sofia Virtudes, takes a deep dive look into rape-victims, and the true pain that they feel after surviving such a trauma. Since we now live in an age in which social media is always present, victims of all sorts of acts are either hiding in the shadows or are out in public, given the opportunity to spread awareness. In most cases, however, the victims of these heinous crimes are afraid of the public response they will receive.

The article focuses on victims who have come out to share their stories and the media and public have twisted their stories and courage and has made them believe that the assault was their fault. For example, some people have questioned victims with questions like "What were you wearing when it happened? Or, "Why didn't you come forward sooner?" This type of victim blaming discourages other victims from coming forward, which makes the victim live in agony with their rapist going free and living their lives as if nothing happened. In fact, experts estimate that only about 6% of rape cases are ever reported.

"To better understand why victim-blaming remains rampant in our society, Torre cited the just-world hypothesis, or the belief that the world is inherently fair and rational."

"If the world is fair, you get what you deserve. If you work hard, you will get good things; if you're a good person, you will have good karma," she explained the line of reasoning. Those who subscribe to that belief think that the unfortunate events happening to a person must be related to their "competence, virtue, or lack thereof." (Rappler.com)

People who resort to victim blaming often do so to reduce their own discomfort from an idea that conflicts with their belief. The blamers say "This won't happen to me, because I know better." [Victim blaming is more prevalent in rape than in other types of crimes because of the dominant narratives on sexuality – men as the aggressors and women as the sexual gatekeepers.]

(https://rappler.com/nation/victim-blaming-why-survivors-sexual-violence-not-come-forward)

Hypocrisy

Hypocrisy is the contrivance of a false appearance of virtue or goodness, while concealing real character traits or inclinations, especially with respect to religious and moral beliefs; hence, in a general sense, hypocrisy may involve dissimulation, pretense, or a sham. Hypocrisy is the practice of engaging in the same behavior or activity for which one criticizes another. In moral psychology, it is the failure to follow one's own expressed moral rules and principles. (Wikipedia)

Politicians are known to make remarks that make them hypocritical. For example, in the wake of the shooting of Congressman Steve Scalise, the President's advisor Kellyanne Conway told Fox News, "You can't attack people personally in a way and think that tragedies like this won't happen." (The Atlantic) However, her boss, the President, is notorious for personally attacking people hundreds of times.

The hypocrisy does not just come from the right. On the left, President Obama was vocally adamant about the importance of press freedoms, while simultaneously waging a war on leaks from his White House. (The Atlantic)

A study by Yale University makes clear why we accept at least some hypocrisy in our politics, because we tend to be harder on hypocrites when they belong to the opposite group. "Dan Stalder, a psychology professor at University of Wisconsin, Whitewater, [said] that people don't typically realize when they're being hypocrites, and they usually don't stop after they're called out for it, either. Instead, they might deny the accusation so they can "stay in a state of hypocrisy," he said. Less commonly, hypocrites might "acknowledge the inconsistency and either undo it or vow to do better."" (https://www.theatlantic.com/science/archive/2017/06/mind-of-a-hypocrite/530958/)

An article in The New York Times covered a story about a restaurant owner who received backlash from his loyal customers after he revealed that he had voted for President Trump during an interview with MSNBC. The issue was not so much that he voted for him or the fact that he was honest about his personal political view, the issue was the fact that his business served as a community hub for marginalized groups.

He had presented his business and himself as a liberal which cast doubt about his character and whether he truly believed what he was selling. It should have been a red flag that the restaurant's name was "Indian Road Cafe" located in a gentrified location owned by a white man. Although the community and employees state that Brosco was very supportive of the community, this admittance was a betrayal of their trust because admitting himself to be a Trump supporter is hypocritical of what he presented himself to be. Brosco states that he has never donated money to the Trump campaign but has financially supported the community. Even though he had created a "safe space" for the community, the community and employees stopped supporting his business.
(https://www.nytimes.com/2020/07/08/nyregion/indian-road-cafe-trump.html)

Propaganda

Propaganda is communication that is used primarily to influence an audience and further an agenda, which may not be objective and may be presenting facts selectively to encourage a particular synthesis or perception, or using loaded language to produce an emotional rather than a rational response to the information that is presented. Propaganda is often associated with material prepared by governments, but activist groups, companies, religious organizations, the media, and individuals can also produce propaganda. (Wikipedia)

When we think of this idea of propaganda, we might immediately picture World War II propaganda posters. Whether it is an image of Rosie the Riveter or Nazi promotional advertisements, these are the examples of propaganda that can help us understand the impact propaganda can have on a group of people. It can also be interesting to think about how propaganda has changed today, we can look at a modern example.

This particular example comes from Quartz, and is written by Annabelle Timsit. "A Chinese propaganda video mocks America's response to the coronavirus crisis." Timsit explains that the Chinese government had released a video called "Once Upon a Virus," where Lego-like figures are used to represent recent power struggles between China and the United States. In the video, the Chinese toys are mocking the American toys for their slow response to the coronavirus. The Chinese Lego figures praise Beijing's quick and efficient response to the pandemic, which paints them as winning, and in a more powerful light. As it is believed that the coronavirus broke out in China, the country has been under scrutiny since the virus first emerged. This children's video is a clear example of how China is using elements of both truth and embellishment to persuade their people that they are the stronger nation. It is interesting to see that today's propaganda is digital (no more posters), and that this particular example targets children, who are more vulnerable to propaganda and are not critical thinkers. This video presents China in a positive light, even though they may be. In the wrong.

(https://qz.com/1850097/chinese-propaganda-video-mocks-us-response-to-coronavirus-crisis/)

Creeping Normality

Creeping normality (also called landscape amnesia) is a process by which a major change can be accepted as normal and acceptable if it happens slowly through small, often unnoticeable, increments of change. The change could otherwise be regarded as objectionable if it took place in a single step or short period. (Wikipedia)

In 2020, rapper Kanye West, declared himself as a presidential candidate. While most media outlets saw this as a likely publicity stunt in order to keep his name in the news, many people took it seriously. Why not, after all. If Donald Trump, a reality show star could become president, then why not a rapper. In 2015, this would have been absurd and dismissed outright, but with a creeping normality that anything is now possible and not out of the question, West's declaration has stayed in the headlines and some news outlets, mainly those aimed at younger people, are taking it somewhat serious.

While the presidency used to be an office of great distinction, with West's pronouncement that he would even consider running for president shows that we have slowly moved toward a world filled with ever-growing absurdity. If West had ever shown an interest in helping people, and not had been a negative force in the media (rapping about controversial and offensive things), then more people would accept the idea of him being a leader of some sort. But with his bad boy behavior, and his former support of President Trump, anyone who took his candidacy seriously has been desensitized to how absurd our world had become.

(https://www.cnn.com/2020/07/08/entertainment/kanye-trump-coronavirus-forbes/)

Slippery Slope

A slippery slope argument (SSA), in logic, critical thinking, political rhetoric, and caselaw, is often viewed as a logical fallacy in which a party asserts that a relatively small first step leads to a chain of related events culminating in some significant (usually negative) effect. The core of the slippery slope argument is that a specific decision under debate is likely to result in unintended consequences. The strength of such an argument depends on the warrant, i.e. whether or not one can demonstrate a process that leads to the significant effect. This type of argument is sometimes used as a form of fearmongering, in which the probable consequences of a given action are exaggerated in an attempt to scare the audience. (Wikipedia)

(https://www.nytimes.com/2018/09/11/opinion/the-slippery-slope-of-regulating-social-media.html)

Cassandra Complex

The Cassandra Complex occurs when someone has a valid prediction of the future, but is not believed for one reason or another. It is defined as "a psychological phenomenon in which an individual's accurate prediction of a crisis", (health experts highly encourage the use of PPE to stop the increase of cases), "is ignored or dismissed", (those not taking mask-wearing seriously and gather for a campaign rally). This concept hurts the world because it makes people disregard specialists of every field for no logical reason, thus putting themselves or others in danger. These dangers could range from the issue of a pandemic becoming worse due to not heeding warnings to the issue of climate change and refusing to take action against environmental damage.

A perfect example is in 2020 when Dr. Anthony Fauci predicted a spike in coronavirus cases if people did not social distance and wear masks. His warnings were not heeded by those in the Trump administration, and by extension many state governors, preferring to play politics rather than listen to the science. As a result, spikes did occur and more people died from the coronavirus. In this case, Dr. Fauci was Cassandra, the prophet with information about the future, but who was not believed when he brought the information to the government.

During the pandemic, it was common to find articles with prominently feature medical experts who were being ignored and dismissed in the wake of COVID-19. In the article, *Mark Meadows says there will not be a 'national mandate' on wearing masks* (Fox News), the issue being discussed is the essential nature of wearing masks, and Mr. Meadows said there will be no 'national mandate' on it. It touches on Trump's personal stance on it, as well as precautions to be taken, (or not), at his campaign.

This all came in the wake of medical professionals across the board highly suggesting masks, social distancing, and in small groups so the case numbers of coronavirus would start dropping in the United States. It's quite simple to observe the subtext in the article that, while masks seem important, the President and his team leaned against wearing them. The article uses very loose and implicative phrasing throughout the article, such as "[he] *suggested* masks *could* be required" (at the rally), and pulling quotes such as "We're a nation of freedoms..." and "certainly a nation mandate is *not* in order". Related articles and advertisements link readers to health risks posed by face masks.

(https://www.foxnews.com/politics/mark-meadows-says-there-will-not-be-a-national-mandate-on-wearing-masks)

Fighting back

Question the Source

Most of us check in multiple times each day to social media to see "what's new," maybe to catch up with friends, or to stay up to date with current events. Sometimes we're just mindlessly scrolling through our timeline when an interesting article appears. Maybe it's something a friend shared or commented on, maybe the headline is click-bait (intentionally sensational to make us want to know more) or maybe the social network's algorithm thought you might want to know about this. What you might not know is where that article came from, you just know it's not something you follow.

When this type of article or news story appears, resist your natural reflex to automatically click on the article. Before you allow yourself to let the ideas in that article into your brain, ask yourself "where did this come from," and "why am I seeing it?" If you can see the publisher's name or website in the link, is the publisher a well-known and established information source, or does it come from a website you've never heard of? The internet has given rise to many excellent news outlets – there are many websites that didn't exist a decade ago, but which have worked hard to gain our trust. But for every reputable website, there are dozens that are not reputable and which don't hold themselves to a high level of integrity. It's very easy for anyone to start a blog, publish their articles to Facebook, and spread inaccurate news stories or even intentionally spread fake news.

Before clicking on an article from an unknown source, it may be useful to first research the website or the author. Just use your favorite search engine and search the website name and then type in "reputable?" to read if there is any commentary online about the site. You could also do this for the article's author to find out if that person is a reputable journalist or just someone who started a blog. Finding the author's bio will give you lots of information—do they have a journalism degree, do they work for a reputable news outlet, have they won journalistic awards? These checks don't automatically mean that the article is based on fact, but it may be a good indicator.

Verify the Story

While browsing Facebook or Twitter, you suddenly see an incredible headline. The article looks legitimate, so you click the headline and read the story. The story is incredible, but you haven't seen this anywhere else. Maybe the website has an exclusive and you'll hear about it soon from other sources. How can you tell if what you're reading is real news, fake news, or somewhere in between?

When important news breaks in the world, especially when the story has to do with politics, the story spreads quickly and is picked up by multiple news outlets. This typically happens within minutes in today's interconnected world. A real news article with new and factual information will appear in other places with its title including the original source ("'blank' is reporting…"). This means that when a website is reporting something as news, you should be able to visit another news website that you have verified as reputable, and find the story being reported there as well.

Beware of the story that you only see reported on a single website or in a single news outlet. This usually means that the story may lack the journalistic integrity common at reputable and established news sites.

Get Out of Your Bubble

You may have heard of people talking about "living in a bubble" or about information going through an "echo chamber." Simply put, technology has allowed us to surround ourselves with like-minded people and simply "hide" people and ideas that offend or annoy us. We also tend to follow people and news sources that appeal to our sensibilities and worldviews, while keeping out sources with disagree with.

The internet is more than happy to help us effectively filter out things we don't like. In fact, Facebook, Twitter, and Google likely know you so well that they will help you browse the internet without ever encountering an idea contrary to what you believe. They do this to keep you happy so that you'll keep browsing and eventually click on advertisements, which is how they make money.

Living in a bubble leads to closing ourselves off to ideas and viewpoints different from our own. We hear about the same stories from the same points of view and from the same sources (the echo chamber), and isolate ourselves from different opinions about the world. This ultimately leads to misunderstandings and divisions with people who are different than us. A perfect example is how some people couldn't understand how Donald Trump could get elected. They were only exposed to one way of thinking about him and could not imagine there was an entire group of people who thought about him differently.

A better way to get your information and news is to anonymously browse news aggregators like Google News or Yahoo News without being signed into your account. Not being signed in means the websites can't customize news based on your search and click histories. As an extra precaution, you can use the Tor web browser, which anonymizes your web surfing and even your location. This technique also works well on YouTube and any other site where you don't want to stay in your bubble.

Recognize That All News is Biased

Something that most of us don't tend to think about is the fact that all media, including the news, is created by someone – another human. Although the best journalists try their best to report the facts as they see them, they are still people with their own ideas and biases. Journalists also need to write stories their editors assign to them, which in turn are written to appeal to the reader.

This means that whether it is a conscious effort or not, all news has a bias. The reporter wants to satisfy the editor. The editor wants to satisfy the reader. A satisfied reader will read more stories and hopefully click on some ads. The editor knows a bit about the reader, like age, gender, and income, and they try to write a story in a way that appeals to them. This is why a news story will be written slightly differently depending on the source. In addition, some news outlets will demonstrate a bias by leaving out some stories and overemphasizing other stories. This bias by omission can be as simple as not reporting a politician's good deeds while overemphasizing his or her bad deeds, or vice-versa.

Part of the reason bias exists is to appeal to a specific audience, but part of it is also to be unique. With news being published online all day every day, how does a local newspaper compete against a national newspaper? Or how can a blog get readers if a big news story is already being reported on all of the big news sites? The answer is to approach the news story from a unique perspective. This unique perspective may be as simple as including details that are of interest to a specific subset of the population. This unique take on a news story is itself a bias.

Understanding the intended audience for a news outlet will help us better understand the bias in that particular outlet. If the audience is part of an older age group, the news is likely to contain stories about politics, health news, and money matters. If the outlet tends to skew younger, you may see stories about job hunting and education. If a news outlet is more left-leaning politically, you'll tend to see positive stories about universal healthcare, immigration and legalization, and social programs. If the news outlet is more right-leaning politically, those topics are more likely to be covered negatively. The important thing to understand is that a bias exists in all news media, and we should be aware of it.

It's impossible for us to ignore news or to completely shut out all news, but these techniques should help us to better understand our world and to realize that the world is not necessarily as it seems in a story on the screen.

Test your critical thinking skills

You've learned the basic critical thinking skills necessary to survive in today's post-truth era. Now go online and test out your new skills!

- Click on a news article on your social media news feed. Can you find any bias in this article that will give you a clue of who is the intended audience? Try to find out more about the author. What does the author's bio tell you about any potential biases or the reliability of the information contained in the article?

- Find an article on your news feed with a headline that looks like click-bait. Read the article then use your favorite search engine to find this story on another website. Can you find another source that confirms the truthfulness of the article? Can you find any facts online about it? If the article seems like fake news, why do you think it was written?
- Visit a news website which you have heard of, but you don't regularly visit because you believe they're biased. Compare the top stories to the top stories on your favorite news outlets. How are the stories different or similar?
- Think about the news you follow on social media. Why did you choose to follow those particular news outlets? What do they say about how you see the world?

Important note: If you find that a friend on social media has shared a questionable article, explain to them why you believe the article is questionable.

You'll be helping your friend better understand the information they're exposed to, and you'll be combatting fake news and false information to everyone's benefit!

Conclusion

Throughout this book, I have detailed ways to teach media literacy in any curriculum and for any subject, and I have also given specific examples of how to use specific types of media to teach specific skills. I have talked about using television and radio to teach us about the ways we interpret reality, just as I have talked about using media literacy to teach us about ways to interpret math and history.

Along the way, I have also discussed the usefulness of podcasts and blogs as teaching tools, especially in helping students create their own media. Empowering students to create gives them the confidence they need in an age where they are fed information and beliefs at every turn.

But I have only just scratched the surface.

There are so many more ways to teach media literacy than what I have detailed here. There are also so many more ways to teach critical analysis than what I have included here. Every day there are more and more organizations and educators dedicated to helping students learn about media literacy. Because of this, there are huge amounts of information out there to explore, and there is always more information arriving every day.

If you take anything from this book, it is that you should not be afraid to try something new to reach your goals in the classroom. There is always a better way of doing something, and this is especially true for the concept of media literacy education. Now that you know the basics, come up with new and exciting ways to teach your students about media. Mix and match activities I have mentioned here to create your own customized lesson plans.

Do not be afraid of going your own way – your teaching ideas are just as valid as those media literacy "experts" with PhDs and dozens of books on the subject. You are on the front lines of teaching kids, and you know exactly what you need in order to teach them what they need to know. No research study could replace your knowledge and experience, so keep that in mind when you decide to implement a new teaching idea in the classroom.

If you take two things from this book, let the second thing be that you should not be afraid to embrace technology as a teaching tool. Technology is there to help us not hurt us. Kids already use technology in their daily lives and it is our job to find out how to leverage their technology usage to their benefit. Kids are going to go online, use their cell phones for more than just calls, and encounter technology everywhere they go. We need to show them how to be better users of it.

If we think we are bombarded by media today, imagine how impactful media will be to tomorrow's leaders. If we teach them how to critically analyze today, they will be better citizens tomorrow. Media are the key, because media encompass everything they experience.

Some Final Thoughts

One of the main goals of this book has been to get you to begin asking questions about the media you consume, and hopefully this has helped make you more media literate. It is always useful to think back to when we began our journey and to consider how your views have changed on media after having read through the material. The two most fundamental questions to consider are:

- How do you view media differently today than when we first started?

- In what ways can you apply the skills you have learned here to other parts of your life?

If this book has been successful in its goal of helping you better understand how the media works, then hopefully the answer to the first question is "very differently." Hopefully you now approach each media experience with a more critical eye (or ear), thinking more deeply about the messages we are bombarded with each day. You hopefully understand that media organizations create their messages for power and/or profit, and that we should be skeptical, but not necessarily cynical, about the media messages made for our consumption.

The answer to the second question may not be readily apparent to you after you finish the book. However, I can assure you that the skills you learned with this book will carry over to other areas in your life that require critical thought. These skills will help you in everything from choosing which fruit to buy at the market to deciding who to vote on in the next election. And although we did cover every type of media in existence, and while there will always be new forms of media that gain in popularity (think about how the Apple Watch is transforming how we receive and digest information), the skills you learned here will apply to those as well.

While you may have already known some of these media literacy ideas and concepts intuitively, we helped solidify them in your mind by explaining them explicitly. Yes, commercials are trying to get us to buy something, music videos are there to get us to buy the single or an album, and politicians will say what we want to hear so that we will vote for them – hopefully you already knew this was happening. But now you also hopefully understand why it happens and what you can do to decide if you agree or not before accepting or rejecting the message.

Hopefully you will continue to think critically about media and its effects as time goes on. Media literacy is a lifelong skill that only improve the more you practice it. So the next time you read a tweet, watch an online video, check a Wikipedia entry, listen to the radio, watch a movie, read some news, or listen to music, think about how and why that piece of media reached you, and decide whether what it represents is something you agree with or disagree with before accepting as a part of your world view.

A multitude of resources exist for those interested in continuing their media literacy education. Appendix A towards the end of this book contains some of those resources, and for a complete and constantly updated list you can visit UnderstandMedia.com. If you should have any questions, concerns, or feedback, please do not hesitate to reach out by e-mail at info@understandmedia.com.

Appendix A – Resources

The following are some resources you can use to find more information about media literacy.

Understand Media – http://www.understandmedia.com - This is my media literacy website. It has original articles, lesson plans, videos, student-produced media journals, a discussion forum, a podcast, and more. Everything on the site is free of charge.

Common Core State Standards Initiative – http://www.corestandards.org

On The Media – http://www.onthemedia.org - A weekly program on National Public Radio.

MediaEd – http://mediaed.org.uk - Teaches film, media, and filmmaking.

Project Looksharp – http://www.ithaca.edu/looksharp - A media literacy initiative at Ithaca College.

Media Smarts – http://mediasmarts.ca - A Canadian media literacy website.

The Journal Of Media Literacy –
http://journalofmedialiteracy.org

Video In The Classroom –
http://www.videointheclassroom.com - A path to critical thinking through the creation of media.

Center for Media Literacy – http://medialit.org

National Association for Media Literacy Education – http://www.namle.net

Media Literacy Clearinghouse –
http://www.frankwbaker.com/mlc

Appendix B: Myths about Teaching Media Literacy in the Classroom

Throughout my time teaching media literacy (and teaching how to teach it to others), I have heard many reasons as to why parents and teachers have not been quick to adopt these practices. I feel that these reasons do not really fit with reality, but rather they are myths that get perpetuated over time by people who do not really understand what media literacy is all about. I am pleased to announce that every one of these myths is easy to dispel.

The problem with myths is that over time they feel more like facts than unfounded opinions. So although these are myths, they can still lead to problems at schools in which the administrators or other teachers have come to believe them. So as I dispel each myth, I also show you how to work around the negative perceptions associated with each one.

"Media literacy does not fit the standards."

Many teachers are concerned that media literacy does not fit state teaching standards. They are concerned that they need to meet certain standards when deciding what to teach, and that media literacy just does not fit right with anything. Teachers also tell me that when they seek out resources to build their lessons that do meet the standards, none of those resources include material about how to teach about the media.

Teachers have also shown concern with “teaching to the test”, saying that they spend more time teaching kids to take tests rather than teaching them the material they want to teach. They say that, unfortunately, teaching media literacy will not likely help improve test results and so there is no room for it in the curriculum and it should be left out.

Some other teachers I have talked to complain about how teaching, especially in elementary school, is so constrained – sometimes there is very little wiggle room when you want to add important issues to the teaching curriculum. If only they had a little more freedom to choose a wider variety of subject matter, many teachers say they would include media literacy in their lessons. This is especially true if your school is following a reading program like Open Court or Treasures.

I am pleased to once and for all dispel this myth, and announce that media literacy does indeed fit with state and national teaching standards! This is thanks to the Common Core State Standards Initiative, which provides a national standard of what all students should know at the end of each grade. This has been adopted by most US states, and the standard includes media literacy as a requirement!!!

I am sorry for my overuse of exclamation marks in the previous paragraph, but I truly am excited to share this information with you. I have had very few "oh, wow!" moments in my teaching career, but this was certainly one of them.

Before we delve deeper into the Common Core States Standards Initiative, let us first clarify that, even before "Common Core," media literacy could be taught in any subject, since media literacy encompasses every single part of our lives.

Beyond the obvious media like television and radio, media are everywhere. That billboard on the main street near your home – that is media. The clothing with a brand name or a sports team that you wear – that is media. The math or literature book your class is reading – that is media. When you lecture to your students – you are media. This very book you are reading right now – it is also media!

Even things you would not normally consider media are media. That stylish rug you bought because it would fit so nicely in your home. The car you drive because it looks good, suits your needs, or saves gas. The type of sunglasses you wear. If we look again at the definition of media, you will see that these things are all media.

Media – a group that constructs messages with embedded values, and that disseminates those messages to a specific portion of the public in order to achieve a specific goal.

In the examples above, you are the "group" and you send a "message" when you buy a rug that guests see when they come over or when you buy sunglasses that "look good" on you. These are all media.

Media are everywhere around us, and there is nothing that says we cannot start thinking critically about everything around us. Think about it. Media literacy can be incorporated into any subject, because the material for that subject was created by someone, somewhere, and for some purpose.

Consider why your school chose the reading program they chose to use, or the math book they chose. What factors lead to those decisions? Who wrote that information and how does affect the way you and your students will observe the world?

Media literacy can be incorporated into any task and into every subject. The most important part about media literacy is to ask questions about the information around us. Information is everywhere, so just figure out the right questions. The most popular questions (and that can be applied to any media, and any piece of information) are one word questions. Why? Who? How? We will talk more about these and other very basic questions you can use to discuss media with students in a moment.

The most important thing to take away is that media literacy is not a separate subject – it belongs to every subject. It involves everything, so it can be incorporated into anything.

Now back to "Common Core." If you want further proof that media literacy is a part of teaching standards, review the Common Core State Standards Initiative, an attempt to harmonize teaching standards across all states. As of this writing, most

US states (45+) have adopted the standards. On page 4 of the state standards document, it states:

"To be ready for college, workforce training, and life in a technological society, students need the ability to gather, comprehend, evaluate, synthesize, and report on information and ideas, to conduct original research in order to answer questions or solve problems, and to analyze and create a high volume and extensive range of print and non-print texts in media forms old and new. The need to conduct research and to produce and consume media is embedded into every aspect of today's curriculum. In like fashion, research and media skills and understandings are embedded throughout the Standards rather than treated in a separate section."

Clearly, media literacy is here to stay, and kids will now be required to understand its concepts along with everything else they learn in school. Not only is there "room" for this in the curriculum, it is actually a Common Core requirement!

"I do not have enough time to teach media literacy."

Teachers often tell me they barely have enough time to teach the topics and subjects they need to teach, let alone any time to teach anything extra. As we saw in the previous section, media literacy is not "extra", but is a part of everything teachers already teach. But the problem still persists – most teachers do not have time to find resources and to figure out ways to incorporate them into their lessons.

Many teachers I know have limited resources – limited money and time. Some of them buy their own materials because the district either cannot afford to buy those materials, or because they do not value the teacher's reasoning for buying those materials. Teachers have a hard enough time assembling the lessons they are going to teach with the limited resources they have purchased, so buying anything else is just prohibitive.

Teachers also say they spend a lot of time dealing with student needs, parental involvement, and their administration. Students demand a lot of time and effort, and figuring out how to best service each student can certainly be a challenge. Every student has specific needs and for students to learn the best they can, teachers must find the best way to teach each student while still teaching the entire class. And parental involvement is wonderful, but I am sure you can relate when I say that dealing with parents is sometimes a job in and of itself! Dealing with the administration can also be draining. Requesting resources from the school's already stretched budget is always frustrating, and can take a lot of time and bear no results.

Here comes some good news for teachers stretched for time. Teachers do not need to teach specific media literacy lessons in order to teach kids about media literacy (although it helps when you can). All they need is to know five little questions that will get their students thinking critically. Once they know these five questions, they can ask students about any subject and about any topic. Teachers also do not need expensive resources and curricula. I talk about each of these questions in the following chapter.

The main point I am trying to get across here is that teachers can integrate media literacy into any subject. Media literacy is everywhere, from the books students read in class to the math and science problems they solve. Below are some suggestions for incorporating media literacy into some subjects.

Math – Try adding up the number of hours kids watch TV on average per day – 4-5, and calculate that on a weekly, monthly, and yearly basis. How about comparing those numbers to the amount of time spent playing outside or with family?

English – Try going beyond the world of story and examine authorship – where did the author get the inspiration to write the story? Is it based on reality of the time, or is it completely imaginary? What do you think the author's views are based on in the story's premise?

Science – Does the material you are reading cover any controversial studies that change or challenge the way a topic is viewed? Why or why not? Most textbooks stick to the widely accepted points of view, but history has shown us that these views constantly change!

History – Who is the author of the history book, and what point of view is he/she presenting in the text? Is the author's view of history biased towards a particular gender or ethnicity? You will find that it often is.

Religion – How do students reconcile religious values with media values? For example, can someone be religious and still accept sexuality and violence in the media? Why or why not?

From these brief examples, you can see there are so many ways to think about media literacy, and it can certainly be integrated into everything being taught in schools.

The best part of the simplicity of incorporating media literacy in such a general way is that you can share resources with colleagues at your school or on the internet. This way, everyone has more access to general media literacy resources that can be adapted to any subject.

You can also consider using media literacy to help advance a point of view. For example, you may use media literacy when talking to a co-ed classroom about home economics, challenging traditional male/female roles in society.

“The administration does not understand its value.”

Despite your efforts, you may still encounter resistance from your school’s administration in regards to teaching media literacy. This resistance might come from simply having a different point of view, or their reasons may be valid concerns that you may not have thought of. Here are some common objections teachers might hear from their administration, and some ways to overcome these objections.

“*Does media literacy meet the standards we are teaching?*” – As we have seen, media literacy does in fact meet state and national standards, including the “Common Core” standards adopted by most US states. Try searching your state standards for the words “critical study”, “critical analysis”, or “critical thinking” – anything “critical” – meaning students are learning to think for themselves. This is exactly what media literacy helps them do.

“*We do not have enough money for media literacy.*” – I always laugh when I hear this one, because all too often school administrators believe teachers need TVs and computers and projectors to teach media literacy. Not true! We all experience media in our world, whether that is inside the classroom or out in the real world. Every student will have access to everything they need to study media literacy – their text books, a TV at home, a radio in their family's car, even the free newspapers and magazines in the community – these are all media! Teachers can offer students homework in which they watch media with a critical eye – yes, you can assign homework in which kids watch TV! No extra media are needed in the classroom to teach media literacy.

"*We are facing more and more pressure from parents to get grades up.*" – Excellent! Media literacy will not only help students become more aware of their world, but studies show that media literacy helps in other subject areas as well. Student grades will go up when They are thinking for themselves and begin coming up with ideas that only more advanced students usually come up with. Get them thinking critically and They will *understand* other subjects rather than just *memorizing* them.

The best defense against a skeptical administration is to come up with some case studies – try some of these techniques with students and demonstrate improvement – and then share the case studies with administrators. Have them share in the solution to their perceived obstacles and you will soon be leading your school in helping to make everyone media literate.

"I do not know enough about media literacy to teach it."

Teachers are often overwhelmed with the amount of work they need to do. They often do not have time to study every new concept that comes along that promises great things for students. Luckily, you do not need to be convinced of the benefits of teaching media literacy, since you are already using this book!

Regardless, it is difficult to come up with a concrete idea of what it is you are trying to teach. Media literacy sometimes feels like some faraway abstract idea invented by people with PhDs that have time to read every single one of the millions of books on a subject and then add their own book! Well, I admit I once thought that way too. I was well into publishing my own media literacy website and producing educational videos about media literacy, and I still felt like there was so much more to learn.

The thing about media literacy is that everyone involved in the community has a different point of view about it. Media literacy opinions differ on a concrete definition, what is included and what is not, and how to teach it to people. But the great thing about this is that you have a support community of people who want to help you teach it to others.

Regardless of this support system, it is still very difficult to translate academic research and technical talk into easy-to-use tactics for everyday use. Well, that is why this book was written – to help you bring the idea of media literacy out of the lecture halls and into the classrooms. Media literacy is not something that should just be taught in college or at universities. It is a basic skill that everyone should learn. But how do people learn unless educators understand how to teach it?

As an educator wanting to incorporate media literacy in the classroom, you need to get practical. You need to figure out the core ideas of media literacy (detailed in this book), and expand on it with your own students in mind. Do not let anyone tell you that what you are doing is not media literacy or that you are not doing it right. There is no right or wrong in media literacy. As long as you can apply critical analysis of media to whatever you are teaching, you are "doing media literacy" and you are "doing it right."

With that said, this book teaches you both general ideas as well as specific ideas. The general ideas can be applied to any medium and in any subject. The more specific ideas (like the classroom activities later on) are great when you want to solidify a particular aspect of media literacy for your students. Everything in this book is a guideline – it can all change and be adapted to your specific situation.

"My students are not interested in learning media literacy."

I often hear from teachers I talk to that their students are not interested in math or science or some other subject they are teaching. They argue, "if I cannot always keep them interested in their regular topics, how can I get them interested in media literacy?"

I often ask these teachers a single question that answers their questions. I ask teachers "what are your students interested in?" Teachers sometimes answer this question right away, and sometimes they take a moment and think hard about the answer. Knowing what your students are interested in can help tailor your media literacy lessons to them.

One teacher once answered "my students are just interested in video games." Well, did you know that video games are media? They fit the definition and they heavily influence students. Why not learn about the video games your students are interested in and try coming up with a media literacy lesson based on those video games?

I offer some examples later in the book, but I am sure you can come up with some critical thinking questions upon first glance of the video game they are playing. You can ask questions about gender roles (what gender is the hero and why?), sexuality and violence, and of course you can ask questions about the implications of actions in a fantasy world and how this affects their real world.

As an example to the video games idea, I will tell you a story about how video games affected me as a teen. I had just gotten my driver's license and I was still learning to drive. At around the same time, a soon-to-be popular car racing game was released. I found that, before playing the game I was an ok driver (remember, I was still learning and highly impressionable in the area of driver education), but after playing the game, I found myself driving much faster and screeching my tires on every turn.

Did the video game affect me? Of course it did. When I was even younger I would have dreams of being an Italian plumber collecting coins after playing a certain video game for hours on end. Did that game affect my life? Of course it did.

You will also find that older students find music very interesting. You will find these students interested in dressing and acting like their musical heroes. Does music affect them? Of course it does. In fact, there is a direct correlation between certain music and violent crimes. Although family and friends also influence kids' actions, music does have a strong influence.

I mentioned earlier that pre-teens watch an average of 4-5 hours of TV per day. Imagine if you can offer students assignments in which they need to analyze something on TV. Not only will they find such an assignment easy (but probably harder than they thought), but you will be teaching them a skill they can use when they leave your class. If you just teach students to read newspapers all day but they do not use newspapers in their daily lives, they will not get it. Teach them to use the media they use and they will innately know how to apply those skills to any media they consume in the future.

I often talk to my college students about media beyond newspapers and TV. Many of my students often find themselves on social networking sites on the internet. They like talking to their friends, putting up funny pictures of themselves, and sharing ideas about their world. Some of my assignments actually require the students to use these sites in a more critical way.

The point of all this is that you should find what your students are interested in and use examples that appeal to them. The more your students can relate to your examples, the quicker they will "get it".

Index

Author Biography

Nick Pernisco is an instructor in the Media Studies department at Santa Monica College, and has lectured in the Cinema and Television Arts department at California State University, Northridge. He has taught classes on media literacy, race and gender in journalism, and radio and television production.

Nick has been a professional in the media industry since 1996, beginning his career as a freelance media producer. He later went on to work in radio advertising, music production, voice and screen acting, and film production. Nick has also worked in many other facets of the media industry over the years.

In 2005, Nick founded Understand Media, a media literacy website containing original articles, podcasts, videos, lesson plans, discussion forums, and a blog. Since its creation, Understand Media has become one of the most visited media literacy website on the Internet.

Also in 2005, Nick founded Carmelina Films, a film production company dedicated to producing socially-relevant video content. The company has produced several critically acclaimed educational videos, including “Teaching Media Literacy: Asking Questions”, “Understanding Media Literacy”, and “Podcasting and Blogging Essentials”.

In 2009, Nick founded TeleBEEM, at first developing educational and entertainment apps for iPhone/iPad, Android, and Blackberry. TeleBEEM later expanded into other app categories and eventually also included a portfolio of online media brands.

In 2015, Nick co-founded Power2Girls, a non-profit to educate young girls in Ghana about sugar daddies.

In 2017, Nick founded Connected Neurosciences, a developer of software for people with neurological conditions.

Nick currently teaches online media studies courses at Santa Monica College, lives in New York City with his wife and two cats, and participates in a variety of volunteer activities in the non-profit and government sectors.

CPSIA information can be obtained
at www.ICGtesting.com
Printed in the USA
LVHW040555260820
664209LV00011B/955